PENGU
BBC

THE UNFORGETTABLE MEMORY BOOK

Nick Mirsky is a BBC television producer. In recent years he has produced a range of consumer and science programmes, including *The Unforgettable Memory Show* on which this book has been based. He has also written for a number of national newspapers and magazines.

The Unforgettable Memory Book

Nick Mirsky

PENGUIN BOOKS
BBC BOOKS

PENGUIN BOOKS
BBC BOOKS

Published by the Penguin Group and BBC Enterprises Ltd
Penguin Books Ltd, 27 Wrights Lane, London W8 5TZ, England
Penguin Books USA Inc., 375 Hudson Street, New York, New York 10014, USA
Penguin Books Australia Ltd, Ringwood, Victoria, Australia
Penguin Books Canada Ltd, 10 Alcorn Avenue, Toronto, Ontario, Canada M4V 3B2
Penguin Books (NZ) Ltd, 182–190 Wairau Road, Auckland 10, New Zealand

Penguin Books Ltd, Registered Offices: Harmondsworth, Middlesex, England

BBC Books, a division of BBC Enterprises Limited, Woodlands, 80 Wood Lane,
London W12 0TT

First published by the Penguin Group and BBC Enterprises Ltd 1994
1 3 5 7 9 10 8 6 4 2

Designed by Gwyn Lewis

The publisher has made every attempt to trace the copyright holders, but in cases where they
have failed, the publisher will be pleased to make the necessary arrangements at the first
opportunity

Set in 10 pt Galliard by Goodfellow & Egan Ltd, Cambridge
Printed and bound in Great Britain by Clays Ltd, St Ives plc
Cover printed by Clays Ltd, St Ives plc

This book is published to accompany the BBC Continuing Education television series
entitled *The Unforgettable Memory Show* which was first broadcast in 1994.

Credits: *Encyclopaedia Britannica*, eleventh edition, (1910–11, from 'Psychology', 22:574)
Encyclopaedia Britannica, Inc.; *The Mind of a Mnemonist*, A.R. Luria, Cambridge University
Press; reprinted by permission of the publishers and the Trustees of Amherst College from
The Poems of Emily Dickinson, ed. Thomas H. Johnson, Cambridge, Mass.: The Belknap Press
of Harvard University Press, © 1951, 1955, 1979, 1983 by the President and Fellows of
Harvard College; *Remembering*, F.C. Bartlett, Cambridge University Press.

Picture Credits: Pages 82–83, 114–17 © Rex Features;
Pages 122–23 © BBC.

Contents

Acknowledgements

First of all, thanks to Mike Gruneberg for his help, advice and guidance in the writing of this book, and to the team at BBC Books – Suzanne Webber, Susan Haynes, Martha Caute, Christine King and Khadija Manjlai.

For those who want further reading on memory, there is a very short bibliography at the end of Chapter 6. I would also like to acknowledge the usefulness of a number of texts that may not be particularly easy to get hold of in your local bookshop, but have been extremely useful to me in the writing of this book. J. D. Weinland's *How to Improve Your Memory*, Ian Hunter's *Memory*, Douglas Herrman's *Supermemory*, David Berglas's *A Question of Memory*, A. R. Luria's *The Mind of a Mnemonist*, Ken Higbee's *Your Memory* and Gruneberg and Morris's *Aspects of Memory* are all full of fascinating information about memory.

Thanks also to the Czech Embassy for permission to use the extract of Václav Havel's speech in the speech exercise in Chapter 4, and to Harvard University Press for permission to use extracts from A. R. Luria's *The Mind of a Mnemonist*.

Finally I would like to thank Judy for her help and support, and Leah and Hannah for sleeping through most of the nights while I was writing the book.

Introduction

Memory is one of the most important gifts we have. Because we can remember our past, we take pleasure from our past experiences, we can avoid errors we have made before, and we can plan what to do in the future. Almost everyone has in some respects a reasonably good memory; we easily remember our friends, what we had for breakfast, where we are going this afternoon, who manages Tottenham Hotspur, that you take/ don't take sugar in tea, and what is important to you in your work and so on. Yet almost everyone thinks they have a poor or average memory, and wishes it was better than it is! Probably this is because we all concentrate on thinking about what we forget – in exams, when meeting someone whose name we can't remember or trying to master French at school. Because of this we forget about all the things we easily remember. But, of course, our memories are not perfect, and the good news is that very often something can be done *by you* to make yours better – sometimes very much better.

This book is written so that you can better understand your memory and, because of this, improve your ability to remember in a host of useful situations. The book will explain how you can improve your memory for names of people you meet, for points you wish to make at a meeting, for topics you want to discuss in an examination, for increasing the speed of learning a foreign language, for remembering telephone and pin numbers, for overcoming memory blocks, for remembering an appointment at the dentist's and much more.

There is nothing new about the main method which will help you to do this – the basic technique was known to the Greeks! What is new is that a large number of scientific investigations have now shown beyond doubt that these techniques really do work effectively, and that, *if used sensibly*, they can help the great majority of people to remember better the kinds of things described above. What is new and different about this book is that while it is written for the non-specialist it is based on a large number of recent scientific studies, and therefore combines a knowledge gained from the distant past with the latest scientific knowledge about memory improvement.

As noted above, in this book you will learn how to improve your memory for names and faces, facts, telephone numbers and so on. Just as important, however, as knowing *how* to improve your memory is knowing *when* to use these techniques and when *not* to use them. For example, you will be taught how you can better remember the names of people you have met. There is no problem about doing this better than ever before. However, it does take some effort, and in many social situations, such as going to parties, there is no point in trying to remember the name of everyone you meet. Ninety per cent of people will probably never be encountered again. If there are people you meet whose names you want to remember, then concentrate on remembering them. Otherwise, if you try to remember everyone you will soon get fed up with the effort involved, even if you are successful. On the other hand in some professions, such as sales representatives, or the police, remembering the names of all your customers or 'clients' is likely to be a valuable aid to the job, and spending time and effort applying memory techniques is likely to be well worth while.

A similar rule applies to remembering facts. It is often suggested, for example, that using memory techniques makes it easy to remember shopping lists. It does! But the techniques require an initial effort and, for most people, writing out a shopping list is a perfectly satisfactory way of remembering what to buy. However, if you are driving to a meeting, or if you are lying awake in bed and some great ideas occur to you, then using memory techniques to remember when you cannot write your ideas down is obviously a sensible use of these techniques. It has to be said, however, that for many people the problem is not overusing memory aids, but underusing them. One case in point is examinations, where far too many people make no effort to remember what they want to say, apart from repeatedly reading over notes. Unfortunately, few teachers teach their pupils about effective remembering but, as this book will show, there are highly efficient ways of improving memory for what you have learned for examination purposes, so that you can do yourself much more justice than might otherwise be the case. Some people think that the memory techniques recommended are somehow 'silly' or 'childish' and that school pupils or even high-level students should not need memory 'crutches'. But not writing down what you know and understand because you cannot remember under stress of exams is surely much more silly. The same can be said of learning vocabulary for foreign languages. The memory techniques which can be applied to foreign-language learning have been shown time and time again to be very much more effective than ordinary rote learning, but I have had a great deal of experience of teachers rejecting these techniques because they look 'silly'. Again, however, which is sillier, struggling to learn the basics of a language by 'normal' methods, or rapidly acquiring the basics through using memory aids?

Of course, nothing works for everyone all the time. Aspirins don't work for everyone all the time and if a few of the memory aids and hints described in this book don't work for you, then don't use them! But at least, if you have tried them out, you will have discovered what is best for you, and the great majority of people *do* benefit considerably from these memory aids some of the time in some situations.

One of the advantages of the memory techniques outlined in the book is that they can work for the young and the old. As we get older, of course, memory declines a little, as does our ability to run for the bus. But the great majority of older people can manage perfectly well to get about, even if they miss the bus a little more frequently. It is the same with memory. Just because older individuals forget a few more names and facts than when they were younger, it does not mean they cannot cope perfectly well socially or that they have some disease of the brain. The great majority of older individuals, including the great majority reading this book, have the same kind of memory problems as younger individuals, although slightly more of them! For the great majority of older indivduals, therefore, the memory techniques outlined in this book will help overcome at least some of the problems that they face.

Finally, this book is concerned not only with describing memory techniques but explaining how memory works and why, therefore, memory techniques are effective. But there is much more to helping your memory than techniques. Taking an interest in a topic, for example, very much helps remembering. Just think how easily a football fan remembers all the football results; again, organizing your thoughts sensibly, so that one idea leads on to another, also leads to better memory. And paying attention is, of course, critical to taking in information in the first place.

Throughout this book, examples are given to help you practise what you are taught on yourself and your friends. For the book to work for you, all you have to do is know that your memory, like everyone else's, can be made to work much more effectively than ever before. If, therefore, you want to have a better memory, you can – this book tells you how.

Mike Gruneberg

■ 1 ■

It's Not as Bad as You Think

You may have once forgotten an important point that you had to raise in a meeting at work. You have almost certainly forgotten where you put your keys down on several occasions. You have perhaps spent twenty minutes looking for your glasses when you were wearing them all the time. You have been to a party, spent three-quarters of an hour in the kitchen talking to one person, and then forgotten her name when you met her again two weeks later. You have forgotten telephone numbers. You have forgotten birthdays. You have forgotten to fill up your car with petrol. In short, you gave got the classic symptoms of an appalling memory . . . or at least you think you have. Why else would you buy a book like this?

It's not nearly as bad as you think, however. Your memory is working hard all the time. The chances are that it is doing a pretty good job. If you stop to think about it, there is a lot to be positive about too. Stashed away in your memory there is an enormous amount of detailed information. You may be able to hum (perfectly) the opening of Rachmaninov's First Piano Concerto. You remember the exact moment (to the fraction of a second) when the enemy on your Nintendo machine will jump out at you, and you can anticipate it. You know all the names of all the characters in *EastEnders* and how they are related to each other (and the names of all the actors and actresses who play them).

Your memory is extraordinarily complex. You expect to be able to remember how to ride a bicycle, drive a car, operate a computer and read a book. You also want to remember appointments and birthdays. You need to remember facts and information, tastes and sounds, people's names and the directions to get to their houses. You want your memory to work as a calendar, a diary, a family album, an encyclopedia, a music system, a filing cabinet and a recipe book. For the most part it does the job very well; but as soon as you find something difficult to recall, you start to worry that it is not good enough.

Some people *are* affected by serious memory impairments. Far more people worry about the state of their memory unnecessarily. If you are conscious enough of your memory lapses to have bought this book, it is extremely unlikely that your memory is seriously impaired. It's probably nothing that cannot be improved by a few disciplines and exercises.

■ **THE THREE TASKS OF MEMORY** ■

There are three main jobs that the memory performs. You are going to need to think about all of them.

★ It takes in and learns new information.

★ It stores that information.

★ It retrieves that information when you need to recall something.

Think of the memory as being like a library. New books come

into the library. They are classified, catalogued on the computer or the index cards (taking in new information). They are then put on to the right shelves in the library (storage). A reader coming to the library and wanting that information should then be able to find and borrow the book fairly easily (retrieval).

There is a play you want to remember, but you can't quite recall its name. You need to check out all the possible ways in which it may be classified in your memory. It might be in your head under St Martin's, the name of the theatre where it is playing. It might also be associated in your head with George's birthday, if you went to see the play as a way of celebrating George's birthday. It could also be linked in your mind to the English football team – if on leaving the theatre you got home to discover that England had been defeated two-nil by Norway that evening. The more of these kinds of reference that you hold in your head, the easier it is going to be for you to recall something of your trip to the theatre. You can use the cues of George's birthday and England's defeat in order to retrieve your thoughts and feelings about the play. And then, all being well, hey presto. You've got it. It was *The Mousetrap*.

George and a national footballing disaster may have made it particularly easy for you to remember *The Mousetrap*. Sometimes you will have to work much harder to establish associations in your mind, or to find the cues that will enable you to recall information. Improving your memory is largely about improving stage one and stage three of the memory process. You can make dramatic strides if you classify material in a way that makes it easier to retrieve, and if you work hard at retrieving information that you know is filed somewhere inside your head.

Memorizing material requires the same kind of discipline as

keeping a tidy desk. Just as you might file your papers at the end of a day at the office, you need to file mentally the information that you want to stay in your brain. It's going to require more effort and more imagination than your paperwork, but it is much more enjoyable too. Your real influence is over how you put information into your brain and how you take it out. There is much less you can do about what happens to it while it is stored there. Some psychologists, however, believe that this is not a problem. In fact it has even been argued that memories are perfect at storing information.

SLEEPWORKING

You sleep for six, seven, maybe even eight hours a night. You let almost a third of your life drift by while you are asleep. Wouldn't it be good if you could put all those hours to more productive use?

In the 1960s it seemed as if new technology had the answer to those wasted hours – the sleep learning machines. Sleep learning machines were basically tape recorders which played while you slept. The theory was simple. Your memory still works while you are asleep. It still records sounds and information even while you are tucked up and dreaming. So if you play end-lessly repeating material to yourself while you sleep, you would be able to pick up a foreign language, learn all those facts you need for your history exam, and master Morse code – and all for no effort at all.

There is no need to make a beeline for the duvet, however. It does not work. In recent years, experiments have shown that you only learn anything if you are lying in bed at night unable to sleep, or waking at intervals and registering the information on your machine. When you are asleep, you are well and truly out of it.

■ PERFECT MEMORY; FACT OR FICTION? ■

In 1959 an American neurosurgeon, Dr Penfield, performed a series of operations on epileptic patients. He discovered that if he sent an electrical stimulation through a specific area of the patients' brains, a number of patients had vivid flashbacks from what they took to be their childhood. One even cried out and started describing what she was seeing while under treatment. She described a mother calling to a little boy in the neighbourhood in which she grew up, and a carnival with lots of wagons and a travelling circus. It was as if the electrical stimulus had unlocked memories that she no longer knew existed.

Some psychologists have used this to support their belief that our memories are perfect at storing information. They claim that we remember every piece of information we are ever given, every piece of music we ever hear, everything we ever see or smell or taste or touch. Our memories are like endlessly turning video cameras, recording more and more information all the time. The only problem is that it is all piling up in our heads, and we have no time to catalogue or organize it properly. So it is all stored inside our heads, but we cannot make much use of it.

If our memories are huge libraries, try to imagine the new books being deposited so fast that three or four overworked librarians have no time to put most of the new books away in the right place. The librarians are running frenziedly around the library, perhaps putting a few books on to the right shelves; but shoving most of the new publications into the nearest cupboard. Most of them are never catalogued or indexed. So when we try to call up those books or memories, it is hardly surprising that we have a bit of trouble.

Whether or not our memories are absolutely perfect is a

matter of academic debate. What is certain is that they are storing a lot more information then we ever use. The purpose of this book is to help you get more mileage from your memory, to use it better.

The techniques described in this book all fall into two basic groups:

★ Learning devices. These are techniques which help you learn material in a way which will make it easier to remember.

★ Retrieval devices. These are techniques which will help you recall information that you know is in your memory, but you are having difficulty finding.

Obviously the two are related. If you learn something well, that should make it easier to retrieve. Nevertheless, it is helpful to think about your memory tasks as either learning tasks or retrieval tasks.

As you look through the book, you will see that there is a range of different techniques that can help you with different memory challenges. There is no one system that is useful to everyone in every situation. You will need to select those techniques which suit your way of thinking and the kind of information you need to remember. It may mean adapting some of the techniques described in this book. There are no hard and fast rules to improving your memory's effectiveness. If it works, it's a good system.

Before going any further with the book, have a look at the questionnaire on page 22. It should help you identify the areas in which you feel you need to work hardest and refer you to the relevant chapters.

■ ON THE TIP OF YOUR TONGUE ■

You are in an examination. The clock is ticking away. You have to remember the name of the man who was Queen Victoria's first prime minister. It is there – on the tip of your tongue – but it won't come out, and the clock keeps ticking away.

You are at a party. You've met the man next to you before, and you've acknowledged him with a nod across the crowded room. In a minute you are going to have to start talking to him. His name is on the tip of your tongue, but it won't come out. You know it is going to appear rude if you don't remember his name (and bluffing could end up being even more embarrassing), but your time is running out and you are not getting anywhere.

We have all experienced these kinds of memory block. At one level they could prove to us that our memories are functioning pretty well. After all, we know that the information we need is in our heads somewhere. We know that we know it; but that is little consolation if we cannot get access to it. The information has been put on the wrong shelves in our mental libraries and we need it urgently.

If you have used a particular strategy to try to remember the information in the first place, that should be your first port of call. Try very hard to summon up whatever mental tricks or mnemonics you have used to remember Queen Victoria's first prime minister, or the name of the man at the party.

With all the good intentions in the world, however, we have to face the fact that much of the information in our memory has entered in a rather haphazard fashion. It is information we have picked up in an informal way. So what should you do?

★ Don't give up. If the information really is on the tip of your

MEMORY QUESTIONNAIRE

This questionnaire is designed to set you thinking about the kind of memory tasks you would most like to improve. It will also point you to the sections of this book that most directly address your problems.

Look at the problems identified below, and assess yourself by giving yourself a score on each of the problems. Give yourself 0 if it is NEVER a problem, 1 if it is RARELY a problem, 2 if it is SOMETIMES a problem, 3 OFTEN, 4 VERY OFTEN, or 5 DAILY. You are likely to want to concentrate your efforts in areas where you score 3 or more.

The third column tells you which sections of the book deal specifically with each particular problem. You can now turn to look up the sections of the book that will be most useful to you.

Memory worry	Score	Relevant Sections
Not being able to remember the name of someone to whom you have just been introduced	....	Chapter 5
Not being able to remember the faces of people you met three or four months ago	....	Chapter 5
Forgetting telephone numbers, or getting them wrong	....	Chapter 3
Speaking in public and wondering why no one seems to remember what you have told them	....	Chapter 6

Having the words on the tip of your tongue, but not being able to remember them	....	Chapter 1
Not being able to find your keys when you want to go out	....	Chapter 3
Forgetting to do things	....	Chapter 3
Forgetting information you need for an examination	....	Chapter 2
Forgetting people's birthdays	....	Chapter 3
Getting completely stuck in a foreign language because you cannot remember vocabulary	....	Chapter 4
Realizing you are losing concentration when someone is talking at a meeting	....	Chapter 2
Getting information about one subject confused with information about another	....	Chapter 2
Finding a study system that enables information to stay in your brain for more than ten minutes	....	Chapter 2
Calling directory enquiries and then forgetting the number you have been given before you have a chance to dial it	....	Chapter 3
Remembering blocks of factual information	....	Chapters 3 and 4
Remembering points to bring to a meeting	....	Chapter 4

tongue, it is likely to come back to you fairly quickly. People are much too defeatist in this kind of situation. There is a tendency to think that information is lost if it does not pop up in your mind within ten seconds. That is not true. Your chances of remembering information increase constantly the longer you spend thinking about it. If the information is really important to you, it is certainly worth thinking about it for up to ninety seconds. On the face of it, it may seem like a long time, but it could make all the difference.

★ Buy time. OK, so you have thought about it for ninety seconds and you still can't remember those names. Try to buy some time. Leave a blank on your examination paper and come back to that question in an hour's time. Get involved talking to someone else at the party. Come back to your memory problem after taking a break. Making a fresh start on trying to recall those names could be the answer.

★ Still no luck? Well, it's now time for what is probably the most widely used retrieval device: try running through all the letters of the alphabet in your head. Think of each of them as a possible first letter of the name you are searching for. This could cue the name in your head. (Have a go at the first-letter strategy in the tip-of-the-tongue tests on page 26. This should show you how well the technique can work.)

★ Think about the name you are searching for. Even if you cannot remember it straight away, you may be absolutely certain that it has two syllables. You may even be convinced that it rhymes with 'Gordon', or that it is a traditional Welsh name, or that it has some strange illogical spelling. Concentrating hard on any of these scraps of information could help lead you to the name you need.

★ Ask yourself questions about the person you are trying to remember. What did the prime minister do? How effective was he? What was he remembered for? How long was he in office? Who were his political opponents and what did they think of him? The more information you have about him, the more likely that you will stumble across something that will lead you to his name.

★ Take yourself back to the situation in which you first registered the information you now need to remember. Perhaps you met the man next to you at another party. Whose party was it? What did you talk to him about? What kind of impression did he make on you?

★ As a last resort, simply try free association. Open the floodgates and allow any thoughts or associations to come into your head. They may be obscure and unhelpful, but they may just surprise you and give that crucial piece of information that makes everything else fall into place.

The principle behind all these strategies is simple. If you can't summon up the name you need instantly, summon up as many clues as you possibly can. It is as if you are on a journey. The main road has been blocked for roadworks. You have to find a route through the backstreets that will still lead you to the same destination.

If the information proves stubbornly elusive, it doesn't mean you have to give up, but you will need to keep running through the whole process at intervals. There is certainly no point in sitting and waiting for the information you need to pop up inside your head. Unless you do something to seek it out actively, you are very unlikely to find it.

TIP-OF-THE-TONGUE TEST

Read down the list of countries. Cross out those countries for which the capital city springs instantly to mind. Many of the capital cities you do not remember will be on the tip of your tongue. Use tip-of-the-tongue techniques in order to try and recall them.

1.	Ghana	11.	The Philippines	21.	South Korea
2.	Denmark	12.	Canada	22.	Belgium
3.	Mongolia	13.	Turkey	23.	Somalia
4.	Australia	14.	Syria	24.	Burma
5.	Pakistan	15.	Nigeria	25.	Ukraine
6.	Brazil	16.	Latvia	26.	New Zealand
7.	Poland	17.	Zaire	27.	Greece
8.	Portugal	18.	Malaysia	28.	Nicaragua
9.	Iceland	19.	Peru	29.	Norway
10.	Colombia	20.	Zimbabwe	30.	Israel

Now, for those capital cities that you cannot recall instantly, try using the first-letter strategy. This should help you find some of the capital cities you could not remember straight away. In order to give you a start, the first letters you need are as follows:
1 – A, 2 – C, 3 – U, 4 – C, 5 – I, 6 – B, 7 – W,
8 – L, 9 – R, 10 – B, 11 – M, 12 – O, 13 – A, 14 – D,
15 – L, 16 – R, 17 – K, 18 – K, 19 – L, 20 – H,
21 – S, 22 – B, 23 – M, 24 – R, 25 – K, 26 – W,
27 – A, 28 – M, 29 – O, 30 – J.

Answers are upside down at the bottom of this page.

10.	Bogotá	20.	Harare	30.	Jerusalem
9.	Reykjavik	19.	Lima	29.	Oslo
8.	Lisbon	18.	Kuala Lumpur	28.	Managua
7.	Warsaw	17.	Kinshasa	27.	Athens
6.	Brasilia	16.	Riga	26.	Wellington
5.	Islamabad	15.	Lagos	25.	Kiev
4.	Canberra	14.	Damascus	24.	Rangoon
3.	Ulan Bator	13.	Ankara	23.	Mogadishu
2.	Copenhagen	12.	Ottawa	22.	Brussels
1.	Accra	11.	Manila	21.	Seoul

■ DON'T TALK YOUR MEMORY DOWN ■

You have started reading this book. That means you are willing to make an effort to use your memory more effectively. And you should by now have been convinced that there is a lot more information in your memory than you ever use. There is plenty of room for improvement, but this does not mean that you have a bad memory.

You now need to dispel from your mind for ever any notion that you have a bad memory. Your memory is almost certainly as good as most other people's. If someone seems to have a much better memory than you, don't be daunted. Ask yourself these simple questions.

★ Is there a reason why this person might be expected to have a particularly good memory for specialized information? If you have been impressed by the way he seems to remember football results, you may discover he turns out to be a keen football supporter. If you have been impressed by the way he quotes from a Shakespeare play, he may currently be studying that play at school or college. He may have just been to see the play. He may have had to learn the lines for a speech he was giving. The quality of your memory depends almost entirely on the quality of your knowledge and interest in the subject.

★ Is it possible that this person has trained his memory, and is using special strategies to remember information? If there is any difference between a good memory and a poor memory, it is a small one. There can, however, be huge differences between a memory that is using mnemonic devices and one that is merely memorizing on a wing and a prayer. Don't be in awe of someone else's memory performance, but make sure you equip yourself with the techniques which will enable your memory to perform just as well.

★ Are you sure that he is really remembering the events better than you? You may not be able to recall everything. You may sometimes recall information incorrectly. Nonetheless, your memory works pretty well, and it is important that you have confidence in it. If you don't, it is very easy to start distrusting your memories. It is easy to start thinking that the other person must be right if he remembers a set of events differently; but there is no reason why he should be. If you are going to start to use your memory more effectively, the first step is confidence. You won't get anywhere if you are constantly deferring to someone else's memory. Yours is just as good. Believe in it.

★ Are you giving yourself enough credit for the times when your memory works well? It is very easy to feel acutely self-conscious about the times when your memory seems to fail you, but these moments are only noticeable because they are so rare. Most of the time your memory is working extremely well. Give credit where it is due. What is more, the more confidence you have in your memory, the longer you will search for that elusive bit of information that is on the tip of your tongue. And the longer you search, the better your chances of coming up with the answer.

★ Did you know that there is no such thing as a photographic memory? There has always been a myth that some people possess remarkable photographic memories. They are supposed to be able to recall the words of a page of text exactly as if they had the book open in front of them. They are supposed to be able to recall perfectly all the details of a map, and to be able to learn pages of poetry at a stroke. It all sounds too good

AN EIGHTEENTH-CENTURY VIEW

It is generally supposed, that, of all our faculties, Memory is that which nature has bestowed in the most unequal degrees on different individuals; and it is far from being impossible that this opinion is well founded. If, however, we consider that there is scarcely any man who has not memory sufficient to learn the use of language, and to learn to recognize at the first glance, the appearance of an infinite number of familiar objects; besides acquiring such an acquaintance with the laws of nature, and the ordinary course of human affairs, as is necessary for directing his conduct in life; we shall be satisfied that the original disparities among men, in this respect, are by no means so immense as they seem to be at first view; and that much is to be ascribed to different habits of attention, and to a difference of selection among the various objects and events presented to their curiosity.

from Dugald Stewart's *Elements of the Philosophy of the Human Mind*, published 1792.

to be true and it is too good to be true. There are people who can perform extraordinary feats of memory. You will read about them later on in this book. None of them, however, has got a photographic memory. They have just become extremely good at using memory devices – exactly the same devices you will be able to start using yourself.

■ DOES MY AGE COUNT AGAINST ME? ■

Most people do find there is some deterioration in their powers of memory as they grow into their sixties and seventies. They may find it more difficult to remember new information, and their ability to recall names of people or of places may no longer be as good as it once was. It is all too easy, however, to exaggerate the problem. In some areas there is no noticeable deterioration at all. Older people remember factual and personal information just as well as – perhaps even more vividly than – younger people.

Memory is affected much more by physical illness and by depression than by aging. If you are feeling unwell or depressed, it is more likely that you withdraw into yourself. You may not be as interested in the new information you are receiving when you are feeling low yourself. In order to remember something clearly, it helps enormously to have a lively interest in the subject. Certainly, elderly people who feel they have suffered a sudden deterioration in their powers of memory should ask themselves whether it might not be a result of an illness or other stress. If this is the case, you can expect your memory to pick up as your morale picks up.

Aging itself has much less impact on the memory than some of the social and medical consequences of growing old in our society today. It is less a question of losing brain cells than of becoming isolated. The more involved you are in life, the better your memory will serve you. Most important of all is that you don't develop a defeatist mentality. If you tell yourself that your memory is fading, you don't set yourself high enough standards and you are too ready to settle for second best.

Age certainly has no bearing on your capacity to make good use of the kind of memory devices described in this book. Anyone can use mnemonic devices. You can start to use them at any stage in life. They will give the same kind of dramatic improvements in memory performance whether you are six or seventy-six.

MEMORY PREJUDICES

There is no real evidence that your powers of memory are in any way related to your sex, profession, address, colour of hair, sense of humour or anything else. Even the effect of aging on your memory has probably been overstated. Your memory is your memory, and that's it. Nonetheless, research suggests that we all *expect* certain groups of people to have good memories, and others to have poor memories.

Women are expected to have better memories than men. Young adults are supposed to have better memories than older people. And mechanics are supposed to have better memories than telephone receptionists. It's good news for airline pilots. We expect them to have excellent memories (and would be very worried if they didn't). But, according to one piece of research, salesmen and saleswomen are not expected to remember things particularly well.

Our prejudices are, of course, completely unfounded. Sales staff will probably be extremely good at remembering the prices of goods on display in their shops, and there is no reason why the airline pilot needs to be particularly good at remembering general knowledge. We are all best at remembering the kind of information which is useful to us in our own jobs and everyday life.

Nonetheless, this is significant, because life can be tough if everyone around you expects you to have a poor memory. If people have prejudices about your memory because you are a salesman or over the age of seventy-five, you are going to have to fight that bit harder to get other people to believe that your memory is as good as you know it is.

■ THE IMPORTANCE OF BEING IN EARNEST ■

Memory improvement techniques or mnemonics do not exclude anyone. They have been used effectively with children, and with elderly people. They have been used to help London taxi drivers master the A–Z maps of the city. They have been used by professors and senior management executives. They have been used to help learning-disabled students. They can be useful to anyone, but they do require some mental effort and discipline.

We all develop mental habits, and those habits serve us well enough for the most part. Much of the information that our brain receives is filed away without us even being aware of it. Some of it is stored unconsciously but, like all well-indexed library volumes, it finds its way to the right shelves in our brains and we are able to recall it at will. We don't have to employ mnemonic devices to remember what we are going to eat for supper or the approximate price of a pint of milk. We don't have to go to great lengths to be able to picture the rooms in our own homes or the names of close relatives. This informal system is all well and fine for most ordinary everyday tasks. If you want to improve the effectiveness of your memory, however, you are going to have to start storing some information much more self-consciously. And that means breaking old habits and making new ones.

You are not going to have to apply these techniques to everything you see. There is no need to remember every single telephone number you ever dial, or every face you meet, or every building on a new row of shops that you see for the first time. You can and should use memory strategies selectively. Nonetheless, it will still require a little effort from you if you are to use these strategies effectively. You are no longer going

MEMORY MUNCHIES

What could be easier than to discover that certain foods are so good for your memory that you need not worry about hard work and concentration? The prospect of improving your memory over a good lunch has always been an attractive one, although the idea of what makes a good memory recipe has changed through the ages.

Traditional memory dishes have included:

● Wear a cap made of beaver skin. Apply drops of castor oil to your head and spine every month. Consume at least one pound of castor oil every year.

● (If you have difficulty finding a beaver-skin cap) Roasted fowl or young hare, followed by apples and nuts, washed down with a good red wine.

● (If you have difficulty finding a beaver-skin cap and you are vegetarian) Use as much cinnamon, ginger and coriander as possible. Try bathing your head in a camomile and laurel leaf potion. But, according to the thirteenth-century physician Arnaldus de Villa Nova, on all accounts avoid garlic, onions and leeks.

More recently scientists have tried to prove that certain vitamins or foods provide particularly good nourishment for your memory. Vitamins B6 and B12 and iodine have all been the beaver-skin caps of more recent years, but there is little evidence that any of them make a great difference to your powers of recall on their own. A well-balanced diet with plenty of fruits and vegetables and some protein is likely to be as good a recipe as any for keeping your memory in shape.

to be able to throw every impression into your head in a haphazard fashion, in the hope that your brain will sort it out for you. You are going to need to file information away much more carefully and self-consciously.

When you need to remember the name of someone you have just met at a party, you may have to make a conscious effort to do so. You may have to pause to think and use a mnemonic device for fifteen seconds, before you go off to the bar to refill your glass. When you come out of a long and tiring meeting, desperate to turn your mind to something else, you will have to hold off for a few minutes in order to run through the key moments of that meeting again in your head before you down your double gin, switch on your Walkman or pick up the newspaper. These disciplines could seem a little bit tiresome if your mind simply wants to latch on to the next item on the mental agenda and is not really bothered about storing the information efficiently, but they are very small sacrifices to make if you want your memory to work more effectively. If it really matters to you to remember that information, it's well worth a few seconds of thinking time. The effort is small, the reward potentially enormous.

■ 2 ■

Forgetting: the Inside Story

You may not feel that you need to improve your forgetting skills. You may feel that you are quite good enough at forgetting already! Nonetheless, it is worth noting that being able to forget information is absolutely crucial. If we did remember everything lucidly and clearly our minds would be going haywire with images and recollections every time we tried to recall anything.

Imagine trying to remember how much you paid at the supermarket on the way home from work last night. Suddenly you would have hundreds of till receipts flying through your brain – not only last night's, but receipts from the week before last, and the week before that, and the week before that. And they would all look much the same. Imagine trying to phone someone who has moved house several times since you first met. Not only would his current phone number spring immediately to mind, but all his previous numbers would be equally vivid. So, take heart. A bit of forgetting is good for you too.

The most frustrating thing about memory is that it does not always behave exactly as you would like. Sometimes it seems to have its own agenda. It will store up endless quantities of information that you have no need for, and will keep it readily accessible for years and years. Then, as if to spite you, it will lose a really crucial piece of information that you need desperately.

You may well remember the colour of the kitchen door of the house you lived in when you were four years old. You remember every line of Elton John's 'Goodbye Yellow Brick Road' (and you don't even like the song). You remember the opening titles sequence of *Blue Peter*, even though you have not seen the programme since 1969. You remember the name of the barber who cut your hair as a child, and you remember everything about the barber's shop (the tubs of Brylcreem, the smell of aftershave, the well-thumbed, out-of-date comics that you could read while you waited for your turn in the hot seat). None of this information, however, is of very much obvious practical use.

Then you try to remember your sister's telephone number when you've left your address book at home. All you get is wrong numbers. When you try to draw cash out of the cashpoint machine, you struggle with your pin code and before you know it, your card has been devoured. If you don't take a detailed shopping list with you to the supermarket, you are sure to forget something important. And you are always forgetting the names of people you ought to know well by now.

If your memory were like a computer, it would be the easiest thing in the world to select exactly what you want to forget. You could delete the entire contents of the file marked 'Goodbye Yellow Brick Road'. The computer might ask if you are sure you want to get rid of this information, but at the end of the day it would always obey your instructions. By the same token you could completely erase all memories of the barber's shop and *Blue Peter*. Then, on the face of it, there would be much more free space on which you could store really useful information.

Our minds, however, don't work like computers. If that is sometimes frustrating, take some consolation in the fact that life would be extremely dull if we were all just hard disks waiting to be programmed. We do remember things that we would be happy to forget, and we will always forget some of the things we want to remember. There is, however, a system

---

MEMORY AIDS

This book includes a lot of advice about mental tricks to improve your memory. If you apply yourself to them, some of them will work for you; but they won't necessarily help in every situation. At least you may not want to find yourself depending on them all the time. There are also situations in which they may not be appropriate. Your first line of defence here might be some form of written reminder (a shopping list, a diary, a calendar) or an electronic cue (an alarm call); but don't entirely rule out the old-fashioned methods. They may be low on technology, and they may be low on brain power; but for generations, people have used them and they work.

● Pin notes up anywhere you are likely to see them (the fridge door, the toilet door, etc).

● Tie a knot in your handkerchief.

● Wear your watch on the wrist of your right arm (assuming you normally wear it on the left), or turn it face down.

● Wear jewellery or clothing that is so unusual for you that you have to keep asking yourself why throughout the day.

● Leave large notes for yourself lying on the floor in very obvious positions.

● Turn the wastepaper bin upside-down.

---

to the way we forget. By understanding the reasons why we forget, it may be possible to anticipate our memory failures better. We can use our memories more effectively if we know what kind of material we find most difficult to recall.

■ WHY DO WE FORGET? ■

Most people expect memories to fade over time. Like an object that shrinks down to a speck on the horizon as we draw away from it, we expect memories to become fainter and more obscure until they finally disappear over the horizon altogether. This theory is called trace decay, because the traces of particular pieces of memorized information are thought to decay in the mind over a period of time. There may be some truth in this, but it is very difficult to prove – and there is also another theory.

Think back to the library described in the previous chapter. The books are coming in thick and fast to be put away by those overworked librarians. More and more books come in, and many of them have similar dust jackets or covers. As time goes by, it becomes more and more difficult to distinguish books – or memories – from each other. What might have been an extraordinarily significant volume in its own right starts to look just like all the others. As a result, it becomes impossible to distinguish it from the others, and the memory is lost or forgotten. It stays in your head, but among the jumble of all the other pieces of information you are receiving, it becomes impossible to recall. This theory of forgetting is known as interference.

It is not easy to be sure which of these two theories is right. Many of the things you forget might seem to fit either theory well enough. If you were to slam this book shut all of a sudden, you would probably remember the content of the last two or three sentences you have read pretty accurately. Test yourself on the very first sentence of the book and your mind would almost certainly go blank.

Have you forgotten the material because it has decayed in your memory and disappeared, or have all those sentences that you have read between the first page and this page merely interfered with your memory of that first sentence? Or are both processes happening at once?

Most psychologists favour the interference theory, but a century's work on the subject has still not given us absolutely certain answers. If you are preparing for an exam, it is wise to stay on the safe side. Your approach should be one which combats both trace decay and interference.

■ EXAM BRIEFING ■

Once you understand why things are difficult to remember, you have a head start. There is now much more that you can do to stop yourself forgetting material. You should now be able to plan a study system that is specifically designed to help you remember the most crucial information.

In the first instance you want your system to help keep information alive in your brain, to prevent it fading away or drifting over that horizon. Secondly you want to make sure that in the run-up to an exam you do not get one piece of information confused with another. If you have a history paper you do not want to get the Battle of Oudenarde confused with the Battle of Malplaquet, or in Modern Languages to mix up your French and Spanish vocabulary.

You are unlikely to receive much help from teachers or tutors on how to remember the information. Although everyone expects you to get your facts straight when you are in the examination hall, you are usually left entirely to your own devices when it comes to memorizing that information. So that means it is all the more important that you develop a system that works for you.

There is, of course, no memory system that will allow you to bypass the need to understand your material and your subject. The first object of studying is to understand the arguments, information and ideas that are central to your subject. No amount of memory skills will help a student who has not mastered the subject; but a good revision system will comple-

SILENCE IS GOLDEN

It does not matter whether it is the Beatles, Bach or Right Said Fred, music is unlikely to help you study for exams. It might make your revision time more bearable, but there's not much evidence that putting on a tape or CD helps your concentration, soothes your mind, or cuts out background distraction. One study of forty law students in the United States showed that they remembered information better if they were not listening to music.

If you were sitting in an examination hall in which music were playing loudly, it might be a different story. You would then be well advised to try to match your revision to the very music that would be playing when you needed to recall a particular piece of information. Memorize your facts to the sound of 'Bohemian Rhapsody' and you may just find that the sound of 'Bohemian Rhapsody' would help you to recall those facts.

In the absence of any plans to play music in exams, however, the rule remains: silence is golden.

ment a good understanding of it and enable you to make the most of your knowledge.

Not everything below will apply to you or to your subjects, but the general principles will. Adapt them as effectively as you can to your particular needs, and also use some of the techniques outlined in the course of Chapters 3 and 4.

☐ KEEPING MEMORIES ALIVE ☐

Make sure the material is well established in your long-term memory. You forget things much more quickly in the first few hours after you have learned them than you do in subsequent days or weeks. If you can get the material well enough established in your memory in the first place, you are in a good position to defend yourself against trace decay. After all, you remember that barber's shop well enough.

★ Break it up ★

In the run-up to an exam you have an enormous amount of information to learn. It may be most effective to break the material down into smaller units. It can be daunting to be faced with pages of revision material on a given subject. As soon as you can prove to yourself that some material – however little – is committed to memory, you will start to feel you are on the right tracks and making progress. There are real psychological advantages in this. If you try to learn too much at once, you may end up feeling you are not making any headway. That can be very demoralizing.

At the same time, however, make sure everything you learn remains in its proper context. It is no good breaking material up into different sections if you are going to have trouble linking them together again. You want these smaller study units to work as building blocks which help you construct the whole argument or story in your mind. If you can do this effectively, your memory of one section of the argument or story should be enough to cue the other sections automatically. The visualization techniques described in Chapter 4 (especially the Peg Method) should help you to remember arguments or long chains of information.

★ Reorganize ★

You can read the same material again and again and again without it really entering your long-term memory. Mere rereading is not memorizing. If you think you are going to remember material by letting it wash over you, you're mistaken. It might stay in your head for a few seconds – or even a few minutes – but much of it will be forgotten by the time the examination papers are handed out. Memorizing material needs to be much more active. You need to seek out the meaning, think it through and structure it in a way that you feel is most relevant.

Once you have read a chapter, run it through in your mind. Write down the points that you regard as the key points. This way you will be reinforcing it much more strongly, and you will also be selecting information and restructuring it. You will be identifying to yourself the sections of that chapter that you think are most important. The earlier you can get to the stage of organizing the material for yourself, the more effectively you will be spending your time.

As you do this, make sure you are not simply preparing a specific answer to a specific question that might (or might not) appear on your exam paper. You need to organize your material by topics, to make sure that you are then equipped to deal with a range of questions that coud be asked about that topic. The First Letter system and catchphrases of Chapter 3 describe techniques which are known to have been used successfully by many examination candidates.

★   **Space out your learning**   ★

Learn the material over a period of time. Ten hours' hard memorizing on the day before an exam may seem to some people the best way to prepare. It is easy to feel that there must be some value in all that intensive effort. Of course, you will

SATURATION COVERAGE

In 1980 the BBC changed the wavelengths of some of its radio stations. Over a period of two months announcers interrupted programmes again and again and again to let people know about the changes. Regular listeners were estimated to have heard the announcement over a thousand times in two months – surely plenty of time to let the message sink in.

Apparently not. Cambridge psychologists Alan Baddeley and Debra Bekerian conducted research into the effectiveness of this advertising campaign. It seemed to have little effect. Three-quarters of the regular listeners they interviewed were so sure that they did not remember the new wavelengths that they could not even make a guess at them.

Unless people actually want the information, or unless it is something immediately useful to them, this kind of saturation advertising is not a very good way to get the message across. Merely bombarding people with information does not necessarily make them remember it.

remember something from a marathon learning session like this; but it is not a good use of your time. Space your learning out, and you will remember much more confidently and for much longer. The more you can think about and organize your material earlier on, the easier you will find it to remember.

★   **Keep thinking about it**   ★

Once it is learned, think about the material from time to time to reinforce it. If you know you need to remember information over a long period of time, set time aside to rehearse your memory of it. Help build that memory up. If necessary reread your initial source for the information, and write down the key points again. It won't take nearly as much effort to revise your knowledge of material as it did to learn that material in the first place.

☐   **MAKING THE MATERIAL DISTINCTIVE**   ☐

When you've got your head down and you're preparing for a chemistry exam, it is easy to start thinking that the information you have to learn about all the elements is much the same. Each element will have a symbol by which it is known. Each element will be a metal or a non-metal, and each element will, at room temperature, exist in a particular state (as a gas, liquid or a solid). The danger is not so much that you forget information about these elements. There is a much higher risk that you start to confuse information about one element with information about another. In the turmoil of an untidy memory, it might become difficult to distinguish potassium from sodium, protactinium from uranium, or fluorine from chlorine. Facts about one element interfere with facts about another. You are going to need to find ways of making the information about specific elements distinctive.

★ As you learn the information, constantly ask yourself questions about the elements. Find out even more than you need to know for the test or examination. The more you understand about particular elements, the more distinctive they will become. You may think extra information is the last thing you need when you are preparing for an exam, but it may well be easier to learn some facts if you have that extra knowledge.

★ As you revise, be aware of the dangers of interference. If you think there is a particular risk of you confusing two specific elements, pay extra attention to those elements and the differences between them. Make conscious efforts to distinguish material that you think is in the greatest danger from interference.

★ Where there is greatest danger of interference, try organizing your revision in a way that will separate the two elements in your mind. Use different coloured pens, or different types of paper for writing out your notes about different elements that you are in danger of confusing.

★ Employ some of the mnemonic devices outlined in Chapters 3 and 4 of this book. These will help you associate particular elements with their symbols and their properties.

☐   THE FACTS OF THE MATTER   ☐

Now, what I want is, Facts. Teach these boys and girls nothing but Facts. Facts alone are wanted in life. Plant nothing else, and root

STORY TEST

The story below is a North American folk tale. It was used by the psychologist, Sir Frederick Bartlett, as the basis of a series of psychological tests on memory in the 1930s. Read it through slowly and carefully (although don't try to learn it by heart). You will be asked to recall the story in time, but not just yet.

THE WAR OF THE GHOSTS

One night two young men from Egulac went down to the river to hunt seals, and while they were there it became foggy and calm. Then they heard war-cries, and they thought: 'Maybe this is a war-party.' They escaped to the shore, and hid behind a log. Now canoes came up, and they heard the noise of paddles, and saw one canoe coming up to them. There were five men in the canoe, and they said: 'What do you think? We wish to take you along. We are going up the river to make war on the people.'

One of the young men said: 'I have no arrows.'

'Arrows are in the canoe,' they said.

'I will not go along. I might be killed. My relatives do not know where I have gone. But you,' he

out everything else. You can only form the minds of reasoning animals upon Facts: nothing else will ever be of service to them. This is the principle on which I bring up my own children, and this is the principle on which I bring up these children. Stick to Facts, Sir!'*
Thomas Gradgrind in Dickens's *Hard Times*.

The biggest obstacle to learning is boredom. If you are trying to learn material that means nothing to you, that does not relate to your life, it is extremely dull. You have no reason to learn it. It does not interest you. So you cannot hold it in your mind. Rather like the shipping forecasts on Radio 4 to the average listener, it makes little impact on your memory.

said, turning to the other, 'may go with them.'

So one of the young men went, but the other returned home. And the warriors went on up the river to a town on the other side of Kalama. The people came down to the water, and they began to fight, and many were killed. But presently the young man heard one of the warriors say: 'Quick, let us go home. That Indian has been hit.' Now he thought: 'Oh, they are ghosts.' He did not feel sick, but they said he had been shot.

So the canoes went back to Egulac, and the young man went ashore to his house, and made a fire. And he told everybody and said: 'Behold, I accompanied the ghosts and we went to fight. Many of our fellows were killed and many of those who attacked us were killed. They said I was hit, and I did not feel sick.'

He told it all, and then he became quiet. When the sun rose he fell down. Something black came out of his mouth. His face became contorted. The people jumped up and cried. He was dead.

Now close the book, go off and make a cup of tea, go shopping, go to a night-club, think about anything except this story. In time you will be able to see what your memory does to this story of its own accord. The longer you can leave it, the better.

For Gradgrind the important information that children had to learn about horses was not how to ride them. It was facts, facts like: 'Quadruped. Graminivorous. Forty teeth, namely twenty-four grinders, four eye-teeth, and twelve incisive. Sheds coat in the spring; in marshy countries, sheds hoofs too. Hoofs hard, but requiring to be shod with iron. Age known by marks in mouth.'

Now this is quite handy information to have up your sleeve if you are planning to become an animal dentist, but it was not exactly information for which schoolchildren might have a daily use. Not surprisingly, the students did not manage very well. The fundamental rule of memory is that you remember best information that you are interested in. You need motivation. It *is* possible to motivate yourself to learn facts that do not much interest you. We have all had to do this for some examinations. Nonetheless, your task is very much harder when you are bored. So don't overburden yourself with unnecessary memory tasks.

If the information you need is in a reference book on your bookshelf, you probably do not need to learn it by heart. If you are going to the supermarket, writing out a shopping list is likely to be easier (and more reliable) than a memorized list. If you need to remember an appointment, mark it on your calendar or in your diary. Don't depend on your memory when you don't need to. It will be dull, and your memory could well rebel against it. Your memory will be most co-operative and helpful when there is a real reason for you to commit something to memory.

□   BEATING BOREDOM   □

We have now moved on from the theories of Dickens's Gradgrind, and no one will be expected to learn in quite the way of his children. Nonetheless, we are not yet in a Utopia where every publication is a riveting read. We all have to plough through dull and boring textbooks, read complicated instruction manuals, and wade through uninteresting reports. We all know what it is like to come to the end of a couple of pages and realize that we have not taken anything in. We all know what it is like to go to a meeting or a lecture, and drift off into private thoughts because the speaker's voice and delivery are so dull. The material may be important and useful – and it may be crucial that you remember it – but it is boring.

FREUD AND REPRESSION

According to Freud, the things we forget may be more than a symptom of absent-mindedness. He and other psychoanalysts believe that we forget those things about which we feel most anxiety. By forgetting certain experiences in our childhood we are trying to erase uncomfortable memories, to repress conflicts within ourselves. By repeatedly forgetting to perform a particular task we may be trying to avoid deep-rooted associations that link that task to a disturbing childhood experience.

In *The Psychopathology of Everyday Life* Freud tells the story of a man who kept forgetting the name of a business associate. Whenever he needed to contact him, he had to get someone else to remind him of the man's name. He seemed completely unable to remember the name. Freud later discovered that the man had once hoped to marry the wife of this business associate . By forgetting the man's name he was repressing his own memories of disappointment.

Doubtless repression does explain some of our memory lapses, but even Freud did not think it was a total explanation for forgetting. So don't worry. You're probably not trying to repress a bad experience with the bank manager if you forget the pin number on your cashpoint card.

There is nothing much you can do about the material itself. It is what it is. Nothing will make it inherently more interesting. It has been badly written or badly presented. Nonetheless, you can do something about your reaction to it. It may not be easy, but treat it as a challenge of concentration.

THE JABBERWOCKY TEST

Have a look at the two passages below. There is no need to
invest an enormous amount of time on this exercise, but make a
brief attempt at memorizing both of them.

> *'Twas brillig, and the slithy toves*
> *Did gyre and gimble in the wabe:*
> *All mimsy were the borogoves,*
> *And the mome raths outgrabe.*
>
> *'Beware the Jabberwock, my son!*
> *The jaws that bite, the claws that catch!*
> *Beware the Jubjub bird, and shun*
> *The frumious Bandersnatch!'*
>
> *He took his vorpal sword in hand:*
> *Long time the manxome foe he sought –*
> *So rested he by the Tumtum tree,*
> *And stood awhile in thought.*
>
> from *Jabberwocky* by Lewis Carroll.

The memory-train is liable to change in two respects, which con-
siderably modify its structure, viz. (1) through the evanescence of
some parts, and (2) through the partial recurrence of like impres-
sions, which produces reduplications of varying amount and extent
in other parts. As regards the first, we may infer that the waning or
sinking towards the threshold of consciousness which we can observe

★ **Argue with the author** ★

If the book or the speech is not holding your attention, you are
going to have to make an extra effort yourself. Just as you find
yourself reaching the boredom threshold, at the moment your
concentration starts to flicker, force yourself to ask challenging
questions. In your mind, be sceptical and questioning. In your

in the primary mental image continues in subconsciousness after the threshold is past.
from *Encyclopaedia Britannica*, eleventh edition.

Which of the passages did you find easier to memorize? Unless you are a psychology student well versed in the jargon of the subject, you are almost certain to have found the first piece easier. On the face of it, this might seem odd. The first piece is complete nonsense, the second is highly informative and full of meaning. In addition it is specifically about memory and forgetting – a subject in which you are sufficiently interested to have bought this book. So why was it so much more difficult to remember?

There are two reasons. Firstly our memories are better at holding material which is well organized. Although *Jabberwocky* did not mean anything, it was much easier to remember the piece because it was laid out in verse. The rhyming helps enormously, of course (once we have remembered 'toves' and 'wabe', we are well on the way to remembering 'borogroves' and 'outgrabe').

Secondly, although the second piece does have meaning, the way in which that meaning is presented is very dull, very abstract. The way in which *Jabberwocky* is written, however, is colourful and intriguing. It gets our imagination going. We start trying to visualize 'slithy toves' (are they a bit like 'slimy toads'?). The piece becomes memorable, because it engages our imagination.

head, start to dispute what the author has written or the speaker is saying. As soon as you can find points of debate and controversy within the material, it will start to become more interesting to you. If you want to remember anything of the event, it's most important to try to engage with the information just at the moment you least want to.

★ Transform the material ★

Remember that isolated facts – facts like Gradgrind's facts – are the most difficult things to remember. Unless they relate to something you are particularly interested in, you are going to need to embellish them quite a lot before they become at all memorable. You are going to have to turn those facts into something of more consequence, and something more imaginative. You are going to have to ask yourself why the horse needs to shed its coat in autumn, and why it has to have so many teeth. Or else you are going to have to picture a horse frothing at the mouth, raising itself up on to its hind legs and shaking its mane, with a huge gigantic horse bit in its mouth on which the number 40 (to signify 40 teeth) is engraved.

Even when the material is interesting, rote learning is not an effective technique. We learn best when our minds are working over the material, transforming it in ways that make it more interesting to us. Simply repeating material in order to try to keep it in our heads is a much less effective way of learning the material than thinking about it critically.

■ *3* ■

Rhyme and Reason

It's got four legs and a tail. You know you've seen it a thousand times before, but you cannot think of the word for it. You see it clearly in your mind's eye. Perhaps it is snarling, held back by its neck collar and its mouth in a muzzle. Perhaps it is small and waddling. It stops at a lamppost and cocks its leg up. Perhaps it is tall and elegant and spotted black and white. You know the meaning of the word. You can see the animal in all its many forms and shapes, but you cannot think of the word itself.

It seems that the meaning is not enough to lead you to the word. You are going to have to think of something else. It is an animal with the first letter 'D'. Somewhere in your head you will be able to run through a list of animals in this category – 'Dinosaur, Dodo, Deer, Duck . . ., eventually you might come to it. Or else you may be able to think of rhyming words. It's an animal that rhymes with 'fog, smog, log, frog, agog . . ., again, you might eventually find the word.

Alternatively you may have very strong feelings about a particular member of this species. Perhaps there is a huge one that appears barking at you every time you turn a particular corner on your way to the bus stop. Perhaps you have your own, or once had your own, and think of it fondly. An image of that corner or of the face of your own pet may provide

SALO FINKELSTEIN

Salo Finkelstein was a clerk whose first job was in a small office in his home town of Lodz in Poland. After seeing a show in which a performer was able to remember strings of numbers and do monstrous calculations in his head, Finkelstein set about teaching himself to go one better. Without any obvious natural gifts, he applied himself to training his memory and the results were astounding.

In the 1930s Finkelstein was touring Europe and the United States performing complex calculations that left his audiences amazed. In the 1932 US presidential election he was employed to do lightning calculations on the votes as they came in.

His technique was simple, although he did admit that it had taken him some time to perfect. It would only take him seconds to remember a number like:

14159265358979323846264238327 9

First of all he would break a number up into smaller numbers. In his head he kept a library of number references against which he could read off all these numbers. Obviously he did not have a reference for every sequence of digits, but he did have a huge

exactly the cue you need to remember the word 'dog'.

To use your memory most effectively you have to be ready to use all these types of associations (and more). The meaning of the word, the sound of the word, the first letter of the word, and personal associations are all ways in which you categorize the word so that it is well filed in your brain. The more categories there are, the easier you will find it to recall information. All these elaborate systems may seem a bit over the top for a word like 'dog', but they are crucial to techniques store of number references. This is how he remembered the number above:

141:   the square root of two.

592:   with a ten in front (10592) this is the telephone number of a well-known manufacturing plant in Lodz.

6535: the repeated fives give the number a shape that makes it easy to remember.

8979: here the repeated nines have the same effect.

3238: seen as 32 and 38.

462:   three even numbers in a sequence.

642:   with a one in front of it (1642), this is the year of Isaac Newton's birth.

383:   a symmetrical number.

279:   two plus seven is nine.

You may never be quite as good as Finkelstein, and it's probably not a good idea to set your hopes on a job at the next presidential election; but there is no reason why you should not use exactly the same techniques. Isaac Newton's birthdate may not be as firmly lodged in your brain as it was in Finkelstein's, but you know plenty of other people's dates of birth. Similarly, you can use the phone numbers that you are most familiar with, times of day or identity card numbers.

for remembering more complicated material. The best memories are the ones which can organize information well and can make the most appropriate associations.

The techniques outlined in the rest of this chapter are techniques which will help you use associations to remember information. In order to make the most of these techniques you will often need to identify key words or key facts that will remind you of the points you want to remember. If you are going into a meeting you may identify five or six points you need to bring up with your colleagues. If you are giving a talk you may need to break your thoughts down into a number of key words which represent the points you have to remember to put across. Organize your thoughts as well as you can in a logical way and then see how you can best apply mnemonic techniques.

Traditional methods include:

■ RHYMING ■

Uses: for rules, facts and dates.

Probably because they were so keen on children rote-learning a lot of Facts, the Victorians produced a lot of rhyming mnemonics. These were published as books for schoolchildren, and were often great successes. The problem with the Victorians' mnemonic rhymes was that they were very contrived bad rhymes, and they carried extremely dull information. They were used to teach children about measurements or dates; but most of them were well forgotten by the beginning of this century. There is nothing wrong with the method itself, and some rhymes have stood the test of time. Think of:

Thirty days have September
April, June and November
and
In Fourteen Hundred and Ninety-Two
Columbus sailed the ocean blue
and
'I' before 'e' except after 'c'.

Sometimes you may have been given rhymes like this to learn

by a schoolteacher, but it does not have to stop there. You can make up rhymes yourself. They are not going to have to win a poetry award. They just have to help remind you of a date or fact. Here are a couple that might help you remember the years in which two prime ministers fell from office.

In Nineteen Hundred and Seventy-Nine
James Callaghan was forced to resign.

In Nineteen Hundred and Ninety-One
Mrs Thatcher was undone.

Now try to make up some rhymes yourself. Make up rhymes to help you remember the date of the following historical events.

1918 Votes for Women.

1564 Shakespeare born.

1985 Transmission of *EastEnders* begins.

1914 Opening of the Panama Canal.

1948 Olympic Games held in Britain.

■ FIRST LETTER SYSTEM ■

Uses: for complicated titles of organizations, short lists of names or key words that have to be kept in the right order. Research has shown that as many as one-third of students sitting high-level examinations use this technique to remember some of the information they need to learn.

We are all aware of acronyms in everyday life. The first letters of a string of words are used to create a new word (or an acronym). This is an extremely useful way of helping us remember the names of organizations that might otherwise be a bit of a mouthful. The North Atlantic Treaty Organization would be much more difficult to remember if it weren't for the word Nato, and the Organization for Petroleum Exporting Countries is much better known as Opec. There is no need, however, to wait for acronyms to be devised for you. If it works for Opec, it will work just as well for you when you want to remember the names of four union officials, or four customers who have made appointments to see you. Let's say the names you need to remember are Johnson, O'Hara, King and Ellis. All you need to do is remember the word JOKE, and you have the first letters of each of the names firmly fixed in your mind. Once you have the first letters, you are likely to be able to recall the names.

If you are dealing with ideas rather than names, you simply

POSH PEOPLE

The First Letter system has sometimes worked so well that it has even introduced new words into the language, for example, the word 'posh'.

When the British upper classes travelled out to India in the nineteenth and early twentieth centuries, the ship journey could be awful and they all wanted to be on the side of the ship that gave them most protection from the heat of the sun. That meant travelling on the port side of the ship on the way out to India and the starboard side on the way back. Of course these would always be the most expensive berths to book. Not everyone could afford them. A new word was coined especially to describe people who could afford them – posh (from Port Out, Starboard Home).

choose a keyword for each of the ideas you need to remember. That keyword should then remind you of the idea in exactly the same way as the name Johnson would remind you of the business you had to conduct with a person of that surname. If the first letters of your names or keywords do not immediately produce a word like JOKE, you could then try a first-letter catchphrase, as follows.

■ CATCHPHRASES ■

Uses: for lists of keywords or names, points for examinations.

The First Letter system can be used to build up catchphrases. For example, you may find it difficult to remember the colours in the rainbow spectrum in the right order (red, orange, yellow, green, blue, indigo, violet). You could remember the name ROY G. BIV, but you might find it easier to remember another group of words that use the same first letters as the colours of the rainbow – **R**ichard **O**f **Y**ork **G**ave **B**attle **I**n **V**ain.

Create your own catchphrases or words to help you remember the following:

★ These elements from the Periodic Table: helium, neon, argon, krypton, xenon, radon, lutetium, unnilpentium.

★ The signs of the zodiac in the right order: Aquarius, Pisces, Aries, Taurus, Gemini, Cancer, Leo, Virgo, Libra, Scorpio, Sagittarius, Capricorn.

★ The names of the members of the England football team that won the World Cup in 1966: Banks, Cohen, Charlton J., Moore, Wilson, Stiles, Charlton B., Ball, Hunt, Hurst, Peters.

★ A leaflet delivery route that took you on this route: along Claremont Road, up Southborough Road, into Hawthorne Road, into Blackbrook Lane, into Springfield Gardens, along Fairmead Avenue, on to Ringmer Way, back through Waldegrave Road, and on to Oldfield Close.

★ The names of the countries that once made up the USSR: Armenia, Azerbaijan, Byelorussia, Estonia, Georgia, Kazakhstan, Kirghizia, Latvia, Lithuania, Moldavia, Russia, Tadzhikstan, Turkmenistan, Ukraine, Uzbekistan.

If you are struggling a bit with the phrases, you can split up the information into two or more words or phrases. This can make a big difference, especially when you have a lot of information to remember.

It is often useful to start your phrase with the first word you need to remember (i.e. **A**rmenians **a**re **b**ig **e**aters . . .). This will help clarify exactly what you are trying to remember in your catchphrase.

The key is that the phrase should be memorable for you. How you come by that phrase is entirely your own business. You may develop it in tandem with someone else. You might work it out entirely on your own. Or you might end up using a model phrase that has already proved useful to many other people (like 'Richard of York Gave Battle In Vain'). If it helps you remember, it is a good catchphrase for you. If it doesn't, you should start working out a better one.

■ MINCING WORDS ■

Uses: for the meaning of words.

You can help yourself remember the meanings of words by brushing up on your knowledge of prefixes; but not every

GETTING TO THE ROOT OF IT

There are certain pages in every dictionary that get extremely well thumbed. Everyone has words that they keep forgetting, no matter how often they are looked up. If you want to put a stop to this, the first step is making sure you are clear about the meaning of all prefixes that are put on the front of words. If you know what the prefix 'super' means, you are half-way to knowing the meaning of supercilious, supernumerary, superfluous, etc. When you are learning a foreign language, it is certainly worth flicking through a dictionary to make sure you are abreast of the most used prefixes or suffixes. Here is a list of some of the most common English language prefixes; but if you think of others, look them up in your dictionary.

super-	*situated on top of something, directly over, exceeding, going beyond.*
sub-	*lower than, subordinate, secondary, inferior.*
pre-	*before in time or place or importance.*
post-	*after, behind, later than.*
un-/in-	*negative, denoting the absence of a particular quality, the reverse of.*
de-	*down, away from, removing or reversing the process.*
dis-	*apart from, removal of something, also denoting absence of an action.*
preter-	*beyond, outside the range of something, more than.*
quasi-	*not really, almost, seemingly.*
ex-	*out, former, or not having a particular property.*

problem is simply a question of a tricky prefix. There are some words which are plain 'obfuscatory' (definition: obscure, confusing, bewildering, stupefying), and you have to find a way to crack them. If there is no obvious way, you are going to have to look for ways to link the word and its meaning. You may end up looking at the physical shape of the letters or the sound of the word. Anything that saves you going back to that dictionary yet again is useful. The shared letters might, for instance, help you think of '**obfus**catory' as a cross between **ob**scure and con**fus**ing.

Maths students confused by the 'denominator' and the 'numerator' (words for the bottom and top halves of fractions) have had a range of different ways to remember which referred to which half of the fraction. The 'denominator' is the bottom half because it begins with the same letter as 'down'. The 'numerator' is the top half because it includes the first letter of the word 'up'. Alternatively you could remember that 'denominator' is the bottom half because it is the longer word, and therefore it sinks to the bottom. One way to remember that 'stalagmites' grow up from the **g**round is that the word includes the letter 'g'. 'Stalactites' has a letter 'c' in it, and they grow down from the **c**eiling.

The way you sort out and define words can be as lateral as you like, but try to find ways to help you remember the definitions of these words.

Haruspex: a soothsayer, someone who predicts what will happen in the future.

Snollygoster: a shrewd, unscrupulous person.

Beezer: a nose.

Slantendicular: slanting, oblique.

Lamprey: an eel-like aquatic animal with a sucker mouth.

■ SUMMING IT UP ■

Uses: for any kinds of number – telephone numbers, passport numbers, bank card numbers, accounts figures, dates, birthdays . . . Particularly for short numbers.

You may struggle with names and lists from time to time, but numbers are worst of all. Telephone numbers are notoriously difficult to get into your memory, and numbers for your bank cashpoint cards come a close second.

The easiest way to learn a telephone number is to find a way of making the numbers relate to each other. The area code is usually quite easy to remember so putting them aside, this is how you could remember the following numbers:

752499 (try 75 + 24 = 99)

623824 (try 6 = 2 × 3, followed by 8 = 2 × 4)

370751 (start with 37, double it, and you get 75 minus 1)

541901 (5 + 4 + 1 = 10, 9 + 0 + 1 = 10)

963816 (9, 6 and 3 are all multiples of 3, 8 is half 16)

Now try to find ways of making these numbers add up:

82864

721307

365465

74028

29101

The better your head for numbers, the easier you will find it to operate mathematical systems for remembering telephone numbers (or other numbers you need). Don't despair, however, if your mental arithmetic is not up to much. You just need to look at the numbers in a different way, and start to think about particular associations you might have with certain numbers. The number 301730, for example, might be seen as the target score in a darts match (301), followed by 730 – the time you get up in the morning; alternatively 73 might remind you of someone who was born in 1973. Any associations that your mind can dredge up are going to be useful when it comes to remembering numbers.

■ NUMBER–LETTER SYSTEM ■

Uses: for numbers that seem to defy 'Summing it up' techniques, or for people who find such techniques difficult. And for keeping a mental diary. This is particularly useful for information you need to remember in the short term. Some people have found it less useful for numbers that need to be remembered over a long period of time.

Mathematical techniques are useful if you find the sums are relatively simple. If you have to start dividing numbers by 17, multiplying by 23, or trying to peg numbers to the date of birth of Great Aunt Gertrude (whom you have not seen for thirty years), you know you are on the wrong track. It's time to try another system.

The Number–Letter system is effective for both longer and shorter numbers. It is based on a code which maps each number against particular letters in the alphabet. You translate your number into a sequence of letters, and then build up a word. There are no vowels in the code, so you can introduce vowels without having any effect, and you are also free to introduce any other consonants that are not part of your code. It is as if you are playing Scrabble but your letters are determined by the numbers you want to remember, and you are allowed to use any vowels you like. You do need to learn a code by heart if you want to use this system, but the relatively small effort of learning a short code should pay dividends for you.

This seems to be the favoured code among memory experts at the moment.

1 t or d   t and d have one downward stroke.
2 n   n has two downward strokes.
3 m   m has three downward strokes.
4 r   r is the last letter of four.
5 l   l is the roman number for fifty.
6 sh or j   sh has a soft s sound that links it with six, j is similar in shape to the mirror image of 6.
7 k   you can see k as two sevens that have fallen off balance and now meet at the two corner points.
8 f   you can see f as an uncompleted 8 shape.
9 p or b   both b and p are mirror images of 9. If the loop of the p were on the other side, it would be a number nine.
0 z or s   z has a similar sound to the first letter of zero.

Let's say that you have to remember that 26 people are coming to the office party, that 334 people work in the whole of your organization, and that your Uncle Fred was born on 8 February 1932.

Once you have memorized the code it is very easy to turn numbers into words: 26 becomes NoSH (or, if you prefer,

BRAYSHAW'S NUMBER–LETTER SYSTEM

The Number–Letter system has been around for centuries, but it is often associated with the Yorkshire schoolteacher, the Reverend Timothy Brayshaw. He was the headmaster of Keighley Grammar School and, like so many good Victorians, extremely keen on facts. In 1849 he published *Metrical Mnemonics*, his verses which were supposed to help children learn lots of facts.

His system was a simple one, although his code was slightly more difficult to learn than the code currently favoured by memory experts. This was his plan:

1	2	3	4	5	6	7	8	9	0	00
B	D	G	J	L	M	P	R	T	W	St
C	F	H	K		N	Q		V	X	
		S			Z					

To all intents and purposes it operated exactly like the modern

NaSH) – i.e. N = 2 and SH = 6; 334 is MeMoRy – i.e. M = 3, M = 3 and R = 4; and 8232 is FuN MaN – i.e. F = 8, N = 2, M = 3 and N = 2.

Now you turn those words into images. You can imagine everyone noshing into the food at the office party (or gnashing their teeth in anger because the food has not arrived). You can imagine everyone in your organization, all 334 of them, picking up copies of this book in their lunch break, or you can imagine Uncle Fred dressed as a clown at his birthday party. It is a very easy and effective way of keeping numbers in your head.

system. Brayshaw had also omitted the vowels, so that vowels could be introduced without having any effect on the code. In theory this could also have been a do-it-yourself code for his students. Brayshaw, however, was not a man to leave anything to chance. His young pupils could not be trusted to make up their own words. Instead he produced reams of verse which employed his system to suitable effect. His book includes about 1500 lines of rhyming couplets, which cover biblical and Roman history as well as everything up to the 1840s. By memorizing this verse it was hoped the children would pick up history's most important dates.

For dates after the year 1000, Brayshaw did not bother with the first 1. Each date has three digits. Work out the dates to which he is referring in these lines. The crucial words are always the second or second and third words in the line.

And FeeBLy, Staines near Magna Charta grants.
Now Lo! RoaR tempests, and the Armada flies.
His STeaDy course, Columbus westward steers.
Rome's NeWLy laid plot fails – God saves the King.
Can aNy MaN of fire like London's tell.

Now try to use the system to make words which will help you remember:

1.641: the figure for the exchange rate from sterling to another currency.

3/4/71: a date of birth.

8621: the number for a cashpoint card.

532421: a telephone number.

266311: a passport number.

This system has a whole range of potential uses. You can use it to remember birthdays, dates and appointments. There is no beating a well-kept diary, but this system can even be useful when it comes to planning out your day. You can't always put everything into that office diary. Sometimes there are appointments, telephone calls and things to do that you would prefer to keep to yourself.

Let's say you had agreed to call Karen at 2.30 p.m. (and it was the kind of call that might set tongues wagging if it was seen in your office diary), and that you needed to pop out to collect your weekend winnings from the bookies at 4.15. In order to make sure that neither of these commitments got completely lost in your enthusiasm for routine work, you might create Number–Letter images. 2.30 (in the code) would give you gNoMeS which might be established in your mind by thinking of thousands of extremely shrunken Karens appearing on your desk. 4.15 would give you RaTtLe which you could image yourself rattling excitedly as you watched your horse come in to win at Newmarket.

See if you can think of images which might help you remember to:

Call your mother at 12.20.

Ring the bank at 3.00.

Go to the supermarket at 6.30.

Watch a TV programme at 10.10.

The possibilities of the Number–Letter system are endless. Once you have memorized the code, this is a system that you can use to help you remember any kind of numbers-based information.

■ GROUPING TASKS ■

Uses: for remembering to do jobs.

We've established how to remember the specific time you need to make a call or do a job. You've completely blown it, however, if you forget about the job in the first place. However many number codes you use, you still need to make sure you remember the jobs themselves.

In order to do this as effectively as possible you need to map out a plan of your day in your head. It need only be a loose schedule on which are marked the events that you could not possibly forget – the weekly meeting at 11.30, lunch at 1.00, tea break at 3.30, finish work at 5.30. If you have a lot of information to remember, a skeleton schedule like this might not seem a great start, but once you have a framework you can begin to fit in all the other jobs that you have to do. You can break up the day into segments and clarify in your mind that there are three jobs that you must do between the morning meeting and lunch, two jobs after lunch, and another two jobs after tea. Then, as you go through the day, you can check that you are ticking off the right number of tasks.

The visualization techniques described in the next chapter might also be useful in helping you remember your schedule. If you know you need to write some letters as soon as you finish lunch, you could – in your mind – plant a huge-scale stamp with the Queen's head on it just outside the door of the canteen. It could be large enough to work as a kind of bead curtain, and you could imagine crowds of people pushing their way though it as they came out of the canteen. If you can make the image of this stamp strange enough and striking enough, it should come into your mind just at the moment you most need to remember it – as you are leaving the canteen after lunch.

■ INTO ROUTINE ■

Uses: for trying to make sure you don't forget where you put things down.

Just as files are a system of organizing your paperwork, routines are a system of organizing your time. They sound boring; but don't knock them. Good routines can save you hours looking for keys, and papers, and pens, and glasses. It does not matter where you decide to keep your keys. You can keep them on the back of the kitchen door. You can keep them in your jacket pocket. You can keep them on the mantlepiece over the fire. You can even keep them in the fridge. What matters is that you have a system, and you always aim to put things in the same place.

A system will not necessarily be foolproof, but it will help in two ways. Firstly, it means there is always a pretty strong chance that the keys are wherever you have decided to keep them. Secondly, if the keys are not in the right place, you know exactly how you should set about finding them. Something must have happened the previous night that forced you to break your normal routine. You did not come in through the front door, take your coat off and march straight through to the kitchen to put the keys in the fridge. Something must have happened to interrupt you en route to the fridge. If you have a routine as well established as this, there is more than a fair chance you will remember what distracted you and be able to work out where you put them down. If you don't, there's a fair chance you'll be fifteen minutes late setting off for work and will have to arrange to get back the spare keys that you always leave with the neighbours for your weekly lost-keys emergency.

■ THE LONG AND THE SHORT OF IT ■

It is sometimes useful to think in terms of two types of memory: a long-term memory and a short-term memory. If you are preparing for examinations, or to give a speech, or to go to an important meeting, you are making demands on your long-term memory. Your long-term memory is not simply a place where you put information you need to remember for the rest of your life (your children's birthdays, how to ride a bicycle, the capital city of Italy). It deals with everything you might need to remember at any point in the future. Even if you are only needing to remind yourself to call someone in an hour's time, you will need your long-term memory. You have bought this book because you want to use your long-term memory more effectively, and all the techniques so far covered in this chapter are long-term memory techniques. Nonetheless, it is also possible that you may want to be able to use your short-term memory a bit better.

Your short-term memory deals only with the most momentary of impressions. As you sit in your chair in your sitting room reading this book, from time to time certain sounds and sensations pass through your consciousness. You hear a bird singing. You notice the light change as the cloud passes in front of the sun. You are faintly aware of a creaking below the floorboards as the pipes start to cool (the central heating has switched itself off). At any given moment, seconds after they happened, you would be aware of these things having happened. Within minutes – very likely even before the first minute is up – these impressions are forgotten, or so irretrievably lost in the memory that they will never be recovered.

It is useful to have a short-term memory. It is a way of filtering out material so that not everything has to be processed and set down in the long-term memory. It relieves the burden on the long-term memory, which has quite enough to do without having to record consciously the details of every creaking floorboard. If you think of your mind as a library again, these are the publications that the librarian will not even bother to try to get on the right shelves. There is really no point in worrying about them.

For the most part the system works well enough. We have no need to intervene in it. Occasionally, however, our short-term memories allow information that we need to remember to slip away. Have you ever called directory enquiries for a telephone number and then forgotten the number before you have had a chance to dial it? Have you gone to the bar to get drinks for a group of people but forgotten the order before you were served?

The limits on our short-term memory are strict. It gets overloaded very quickly and starts to sort out information as soon as that happens. As far as numbers are concerned, people tend to be able to manage to hold about seven digits. There is some variation from person to person, but very few people will find five digits a problem, and most people will be floundering with more than nine.

Test yourself with numbers laid out below. Try them one by one. Read a number out loud (at the same kind of speed as the voice of directory enquiries), then cover it up and run the number through in your head to see how well you remember it.

53492
34820

584920
210948

1983107
2829196

67291027
91928254

379013892
048293647

3492019438
7561094856

If you want to improve your performance at remembering these numbers, you need to work at reorganizing them. Instead of memorizing them as seven or eight distinct digits, restructure the numbers in your head so you are thinking of groups of numbers together. Just as it is easier to remember that drinks order when you have sorted it out into 5 whiskies, 4 orange juices, 3 pints of lager and a packet of crisps, if you can group numbers together they will be easier to remember. Try the same tests when you are thinking of the numbers in twos – 32–91–07–46–32, or in threes 219–638–452. It should be possible for your memory to hold more information if you group the information in this way.

■ TALL STORIES ■

The whole of this chapter has been about what you can do to organize material in ways that make it easier to recall. This involves you making an effort to structure your thoughts in ways that might not, at first, seem obvious. You do this consciously in a planned way, and you are then able to recall your information.

GROUPING TEST

Try to remember the following three lists of objects. First:

chair	bat	coat
shoe	salt	ball
knife	coffee	fork
cup	saucer	dustpan
hat	paper	tea
brush	table	pepper
pencil	sock	

This may well seem difficult to you, but as you start to study the list you may discover that the task is only half as difficult as you first thought. Although it looks as if you are having to learn twenty separate words, the words will group together in pairs in your mind. The association between cup and saucer is so strong that you only need to remember one of them to remember the other. It means you effectively have two chances to remember each word. That should have made it easier. Now try the second list.

wren	plate	strawberry
computer	antelope	bowl
zebra	camera	elephant
banana	grape	video recorder
record player	radio	peach
melon	giraffe	dog
Walkman	teacup	

Sometimes, however, you will find that your memory does this for you almost automatically (like in the test above). This is all well and fine up to a point, but you should be aware that your memory does not always make a perfect job of it. Remember the story you read in the last chapter. Now's the

On the face of it, this list is much harder. It seems as if you have twenty completely disconnected objects. If you struggled with it, try again, but this time reorganize the list in your head. Classify the objects you need to remember. There are six animals, five fruits, six items that you would buy from an electrical retailers, and three pieces of crockery. Once you have reorganized the information it should be much easier to remember it. It will help particularly with the recall, because you will know exactly what you are looking for.

Now move on to the third list. This time think about grouping the information before you memorize it. There are a number of different ways in which you could categorize this material. There are no right or wrong ways.

plant	telephone	biro
sofa	biscuits	carpet
television	chair	paper
soccer	bookends	lounge
comic	tape recorder	crisps
confectionary	letters	lamp
stamps	cricket	

time to try to recall it. Take out a piece of paper and write down the story in as much detail as you can remember. Then compare your version of the story with the original on pages 46–47), and read on.

If your story is exactly the same as the original, you have an

MEANINGS TEST

Try to remember the following two lists. Give yourself thirty seconds on each of them, memorizing the items in any order you find helpful. First the letters.

L T N T R G E E O U F B A

How did you do? Six is average. Eight correct letters is good. More than eight is very good. Don't worry if you didn't do too well. You'll be able to do a lot better if you work at the techniques described in this chapter. Now on to the words.

ETERNALLY
IS
CAKES
DAY
BLOSSOMS
AWAY
MEMORY
MELODY
BUT
PINK
LIKE
REIGN
RUN
A
BUT
WILL

extremely faithful memory. It is much more likely that your memory has begun to cheat a little. Your story probably reads much more like a European folk story than a North American Indian story. The chances are that the names of places have been changed or lost completely. If you waited long enough the ghosts could well have gone from your version completely

Visually striking words like BLOSSOMS, CAKES and PINK are the most likely to have made an impression. LIKE, AWAY, BUT and IS are much more likely to have been forgotten. Eight is still a good score for this test. Above ten is very good.

As they were laid out, the letters and words were a bit of a jumble, difficult to remember because they seemed arbitrary and disconnected. If you are keen to improve your memory performance, however, you have to be ready to reorganize informtion, to put it in an order that is more memorable for you. Now you could have shuffled up the letters to find the word UNFOR-GETTABLE, or you could have reorganized the words to make:

BLOSSOMS WILL RUN AWAY,
CAKES REIGN BUT A DAY,
BUT MEMORY LIKE MELODY
IS PINK ETERNALLY.

(from *The Complete Poems of Emily Dickinson*, ed. Thomas H. Johnson.)

To have found the word 'unforgettable' or the poem in thirty seconds would have been tough even for a crossword fanatic who is good at thinking in this way. You could, however, have grouped the letters more crudely. It would not take very long to have found GREEN and LOFT (and that would have only left you having to remember BATU). Alternatively, you might have been able to string some simple phrases together from the words in the second list (CAKES LIKE ETERNALLY PINK BLOS-SOMS, or MEMORY WILL RUN AWAY). This would have made is easier for you to remember more information.

(or at least their role will have changed). 'Canoes' may well have become 'boats', 'paddling' have turned into 'rowing', and the whole tone of the story could have changed considerably.

For those of you who have not done the exercise, here's what one person came up with:

Four men came down to the water. They were told to get into the boats and to take arms with them. They inquired, 'What arms?' and were answered, 'Arms for battle.' When they came to the battlefield, they heard a great noise and shouting, and a voice said, 'The black man is dead.' And he brought them to the place where they were and laid on the ground. And he foamed at the mouth.

Compare this with the story on pages 46–47. It is not simply a question of the second piece being much shorter. The story has been quite distinctly changed in this reader's mind. We are not used to ghosts that paddle upstream in a canoe, so they are turned into men. We are much more familiar with stories in which people are foaming at the mouth, than with black objects coming out of people's mouths. The reader's memory has reorganized the narrative in order to make it easier to remember. It has been adapted to fit a more familiar culture. Once the changes have been made, it seems more logical and is therefore easier to remember.

So, be wary. Your memory does not operate as a kind of clinical filing system. Things don't always come out looking exactly the same as when they went in. If they are left in the memory long enough, they may end up being quite significantly changed.

■ *4* ■

Picture Power

Thinking back to childhood, the first memories that strike most people have something in common. Maybe you remember the sand and the sandcastles (and the sand that seemed to keep getting in the sandwiches) on a day trip to Morecambe when you were five. You might remember a school classroom, sunlight filtering through the leaded window, a teacher droning on and on at the front of the room, while you and your friend made rather unsuccessful attempts at origami just underneath the desk top. You might remember a pet rabbit, the face of your grandmother when you'd done something wrong, the apple tree in the garden or a picture of your favourite rock star that you got free when you sent away eight coupons from your cereal packets. What all these memories have in common is that they are visual, and visual images are the ones which stay with most of us longest.

As J. M. Barrie, author of *Peter Pan*, said, 'God gave us memory so that we might have roses in December.'

Before you starting thinking you can also remember the sound of your father's voice, or the smell of chips deep-frying in the kitchen, other sense impressions are also important; but, for most people, not as important as images.

The previous chapter has outlined some of the techniques

that will help you organize information. Some of these techniques play on the sound of the words, some on the spelling, and some on the word's associations. This chapter is about ways in which you can create pictures in your head that will help you remember information.

These methods are effective for two reasons. In the first instance, the concentration that you invest in trying to think of a good image is in itself helping you to remember the information. Secondly the image, if it is sufficiently striking, should make such an impression on your mind that it is difficult to forget.

■ THINK GRAPHICALLY ■

We are all familiar with charts and diagrams. We see them every day in newspapers, books, on computer screens, and in underground train stations. Some may be complex, but mostly they are very good at simplifying information. If they are good at communicating information from the printed page to you, they are also good at communicating with your memory. Your memory likes simple, well-designed packages of information. It is not necessary for everything to be remembered in words and sentences.

The kind of graphic images you employ will depend on you. You may want to turn your images into strip cartoon stories in your head. You may want to fill them with lots of people you know. It is your decision. The best way is the way your memory finds easiest to remember; but there are three basic rules which should help make them more effective.

★ Make them images of real concrete objects.

KIM'S GAME

One of the most popular memory games is known as Kim's Game. In order to play it, you need a group of people. One person goes out of the room, takes a tray and puts fifteen different objects on the tray. The objects should be very familiar household objects, but they should all be different. You could include a fork, a plate, a salt cellar, a coin, a pair of scissors, a miniature screwdriver, etc. When the objects have been laid out, they are covered with a cloth.

The tray is now brought back into the room, where contestants are given just thirty seconds to look at the objects. When the thirty seconds are up, the cloth is put back over the objects. All contestants are then given pencils and paper and have to write down the names of as many objects as they can remember.

Turn to pages 82–83 and try this game yourself. You will almost certainly find it more difficult than it sounds. There is, however, a way of improving your score dramatically.

By instinct most people make the mistake of concentrating very hard on one object (naming and renaming it in their heads 'pair of scissors . . . pair of scissors . . . pair of scissors') in the hope that this will drive it into their memories. If you do this, however, you are very unlikely to remember all the objects. You are separating out all the objects and converting them into words, but you don't need to do this. You can afford to have much more confidence in your visual memory. You will do much better if you look at the whole tray and at all the objects together, and don't even try to name them until it comes to recalling them. If you weren't too successful the first time, try it again this way.

★ Do anything to make them striking and memorable.

★ Make sure they are dynamic. Static pictures won't tell you nearly as much as moving images.

■ IMAGES FOR ABSTRACT WORDS ■

It is easy enough to think of a concrete image for the word dog, or pigeon, or chocolate; but a lot of the information we need to remember is not always that easily visualized. If you are preparing for an exam or a meeting, you may need to remember abstract concepts or percentages or people's names. At first it may seem very difficult to visualize words like inflation, meeting and profit.

To find images for words like these, you need to think laterally. You need to be ready to transform the words into physical objects that might remind you of them.

Inflation could be the image of a huge 'balloon' filling up with air. If it were appropriate you might make it a 'balloon' in the shape of the Chancellor of the Exchequer. A 'meeting' might be a 'meat-tin' which you open up to discover a huge grilled steak inside it. 'Profit' might be converted into 'prophet' and you could imagine a biblical character in open-toed sandals preaching to City workers as they cross London Bridge in their bowler hats.

Do not feel inhibited about the images you are creating. No one except you will ever know you are thinking about them. The wilder they are, the more likely you are to remember them. Try to think of images for the following words.

Partnership

Environment

Potential

Interest (as in interest payments)

Mortgage

■ LANGUAGE LEARNING ■

You may have found yourself at the bottom of the Eiffel Tower struggling to remember a few words of French from your schooldays, or found that you were not communicating all that well on your holiday to Italy in spite of the Italian phrase book. Language learning is not easy, and it can be difficult to remember words in the language you are trying to use or learn.

You can learn vocabulary (and some basic aspects of grammar such as the gender of a word) much more easily by creating pictures in your mind that link the foreign word with the English word. This technique will not make you a fluent Spanish or German speaker in itself, but it will enable you to increase your vocabulary very much more quickly. Once you have got the words, you are well on the way.

Take the following Japanese words. You will need to picture each image in your mind's eye for about ten seconds, and then test yourself on the words. You should then find that the word has been well established in your memory. Research on this technique has shown it to be two to three times more effective than rote learning.

Batah (means 'butter')

Imagine you are battering your butter.

Gohan (means 'cooked rice')

Imagine you should 'go hang' if you don't like rice.

Satoh (means 'sugar')

Imagine you sat on some sugar.

Su (means 'vinegar')

Imagine you sue the vinegar makers for making bad vinegar.

Kani (means 'crab')

> Imagine asking, 'Can he eat crab?' or a canny Scotsman eating crabs.

Masu (means 'trout')

> Imagine eating a massive trout.

Ahiru (means 'duck')

> Imagine making a duck into a hero.

Kaki (means 'oyster')

> Imagine a car key cut from an oyster shell.

■ LINKING WORDS ■

It is possible that a single image might do the trick for you some of the time; but very often you are trying to memorize material that is far too complex to be encapsulated in one image. You need to remember a complex argument, a chain of information or a list of facts. It would not be very much use remembering two or three striking images if the rest of the information was going to be forgotten.

The only way in which you can insure against a rather patchy recall of images is to link images together. There are three main ways in which you can do this. You will have to decide which one you think suits your purposes best.

□ PEG METHOD □

This is a system for linking together disparate objects or pieces of information. It might be a way of organizing a list of things you had to do through the course of a day – shopping, repairs, meetings, etc. It could also be useful if you are seeing someone and you know you have to bring up a number of specific but separate points, or if you need to remember a series of points for an examination. One of the main advantages of this system is that it will enable you to remember key points in a specific order.

The Peg method is the most popular and frequently used of these systems. You start by learning a code which will provide you with an image for every number from one to ten. One system links each number to an image that is a similar shape to the number (so 1 is a candle, 2 is a swan, 3 is a fork with three spikes, etc). The most common system, however, links the numbers to rhyming objects. In order to remember your code, you need to start by learning this rhyme:

ONE – BUN

TWO – SHOE

THREE – TREE

FOUR – DOOR

FIVE – HIVE

SIX – BRICKS

SEVEN – HEAVEN

EIGHT – GATE

NINE – WINE

TEN – HEN

One you have learned these rhymes you imagine ways to link your first image with the number one (or bun), your second image with the number two (or shoe), and so on, until you

SHERESHEVSKI

From the outset it was remarkable that Shereshevski was able to remember a random sequence of over fifty numbers in less than three minutes, and then recall them perfectly; but the distinctive feature of his memory was the fact that he was able to recall things he learned years earlier. In June 1936, while giving a memory performance, he was asked to remember a sequence of over fifty nonsense syllables (ma va na sa na va na sa na ma, etc). Not only did he remember them for that performance perfectly; eight years later he was able to produce them in the correct order again.

The secret of Shereshevski was that he was very adept first at organizing the information, then at visualizing it. In principle, his techniques were, however, only the same techniques that *you* can and should try to use when trying to remember information. They were the same as the techniques that have been laid out in this chapter. This is how he set about memorizing those nonsense syllables:

My landlady (MAVA), whose house in Slizkaya Street I stayed at while I was in Warsaw, was leaning out of a window that opened on to a courtyard. With her left hand she was pointing inside, toward the room (NASA – from Russian word "nasha" meaning "we" or "our place"); while with her right she was making some negative gesture (NAVA – Yiddish expression meaning "no") to a Jew, an old-clothes man, who was standing in the yard with a sack slung over his right shoulder. It was as though she were saying to him: "No, nothing for sale." By this time the old-clothes man had already left the yard and was standing on the street near the gate to the house. Bewildered, he lifted his hands in a gesture of dismay, remembering that the landlady had said "we" (NASA) had nothing to sell him. At the same time he was pointing to a full-breasted woman, a wet nurse who was standing nearby (Yiddish for wet nurse is A N'AM). Just then a man who was passing by became indignant with him and said "Vai" (VA), which is to say, it's shameful for an old Jew to look on at

a woman nursing a baby . . .'
(from A. R. Luria's *The Mind of a Mnemonist*.)

The story continues in this vein. The Story method is used to link up and remember material that, on the face of it, would seem almost impossible to remember. Shereshevski, however, had developed a way of thinking and responding that produced images and pictures for everything he heard. The only way he could process information was to visualize it, and he generated images with unrivalled speed and vitality. Creating images in his mind became a reflex action. Even when he heard the most abstract of noises a picture would immediately form in his mind.

Presented with a tone pitched at 250 cycles per second and having an amplitude of 64 decibels, S. saw a velvet cord with fibers jutting out on all sides. The cord was tinged with delicate pleasant pink-orange hue.

Presented with a tone pitched at 500 cycles per second and having an amplitude of 100 decibels, he saw a streak of lightning splitting the heavens in two. When the intensity of the sound was lowered to 74 decibels, he saw a dense orange color which made him feel as though a needle had been thrust into his spine. Gradually this sensation diminished.
(from A. R. Luria's *The Mind of a Mnemonist*.)

You will never be able to visualize quite like Shereshevski, but don't get too worried about this. His extraordinary use of memory brought him little joy. You may worry about how much you forget. Shereshevski could be thrown into acute panic by his inability to forget images. And those images could be so vivid that they were easily confused with real life. His pulse would race if he imagined he was running for a train. His temperature would rise if he imagined he was touching a hot oven door. He lived so much inside his head, or inside his memory, that to many people he appeared slow or awkward. The associations that he held in his mind were so powerful that he found it extremely difficult to keep to the point when he was having a conversation.

have all your images filed away. If the links that you make are sufficiently striking it should be easy to remember them.

Let's say you are going to a meeting at which you will have to discuss the impact of inflation on your company, a recent meeting with your German colleague Herr Dreyer, the possibility of Dolphin Ltd making a rival bid for a piece of land your company is hoping to purchase, etc. You have already decided on the images you are going to use. They are:

1. BALLOON

2. HAIRDRIER

3. DOLPHIN

4. TOWEL

5. FLOWER

6. GYMNASIUM

7. SHOES

8. POLICE

9. GLASSES

10. PUMPKIN

Now try to use the rhyme to help you remember this list of words. You could picture a BALLOON up in the sky in the shape of a Chelsea BUN, a HAIRDRIER in the shape of a SHOE, DOLPHINS biting fruit off an underwater TREE, a huge TOWELling DOOR behind which is a bee HIVE made of FLOWERs. Inside a GYMNASIUM you see a weight training circuit where everyone is using BRICKS. Weightlifters are lifting bricks. People doing press-ups have bricks placed on their backs. You then see two large feet in SHOES climbing a ladder up to HEAVEN, a GATE made entirely of POLICE truncheons and helmets, a pyramid of WINE GLASSES with the wine being poured into the top glass and overflowing to fill the glasses beneath it, and a HEN laying its eggs inside a PUMPKIN which has already been scooped out and turned into a Hallowe'en lantern.

The main advantages of this system:

★ Relative to other systems, it is quick. You know exactly what you have to do with your images, and you can create a picture quickly. There is some research which supports the theory that this is the best system to use if you are under pressure for time.

★ If you are using this to run through a list of points, you always know where you are. When you are thinking about bricks, you are on point number six. From this you can work out exactly how far you have to go. By the same token, you have the facility to recall key points out of sequence. If you were to ask yourself what is point seven or point four, you should be able to remember instantly. You would not need to start at the beginning of the rhyme again. You would just think of heaven and of the door.

The main disadvantages of this system:

★ If you are trying to remember a lot of different lists of similar information, there is a small risk of confusion. If you are going into a series of examinations and have used this technique for a number of papers, you may have to work your way through a number of different sets of images. At the end of the day, it is likely that common sense should help you work out whether you want the shoe-shaped house or the shoe key-ring or the chocolate shoe for any particular essay; but you would need to be on the lookout for possible confusions.

★ After creating fifty sets of images involving buns and shoes, you may start to find you are producing less distinctive images. Some people will continue to find the system works for them, but it is possible you will want to try using a different system or a different number code for a while.

Have a go at remembering these words using the Peg method:

1. SALAD

2. GOLDFISH

3. TYPEWRITER

4. SOUP

5. TOMATO

6. TROUT

7. BLANKET

8. CEREAL

9. PERFUME

10. BICYCLE

☐   **THE LOCI SYSTEM**   ☐

The Loci system is one of the oldest mnemonic systems (see Simonides on page 94); but the fact that it was being used two thousand years ago does not mean that it is out of date.

Like the Peg method, this system provides a prearranged plan in which you can place your images. Unlike the Peg system, you are not tied to forcing associations between bits of food or clothing and your memory images. The framework you use is a 'locus' or a place that is familiar to you.

You should first learn ten specific locations. These could be different places in different rooms in your house or flat. Once these places are clearly established in your mind, you have a framework. These places work like the rhyming words of the Peg method. You are now in a position to locate each of your keywords in one of these established places.

For instance, you walk in through the front door, and you can hardly believe your eyes. There, in the middle of the hall, the umbrella stand is floating. It is being held up by an enormous BALLOON. As you move on through the hall into the kitchen, there is an 'out of order' sign on the cooker and there is a strange noise. You see someone is trying to cook omelettes using the hot air method. They are cooking with a HAIRDRIER. You glance up to the goldfish bowl, and you are stunned to see that a baby DOLPHIN has replaced the goldfish. You walk into the dining room. The curtains are down. They have been replaced with the set of TOWELs you were given for Christmas two years ago. Although the towels are big, they hardly stretch half-way down the window, and look very odd. What is more, the fireplace has been taken out and in its place someone has planted FLOWERs. You move on into the sitting room and discover people jumping up and down on the sofa, lifting up weights, and doing press-ups, just as if the place was a GYMNASIUM. And their SHOES, very dirty shoes, are leaving mudprints all over your furniture. As you turn to go up the stairs a POLICEman is coming down the steps. He is taking notes, but does not appear to be in the

SIMONIDES

or The origins of the Loci system

The poet Simonides earned his living by writing and performing poems for Greek noblemen. Towards the end of one particular banquet, for which he had composed a poem in praise of a man named Scopas of Thessaly, Simonides was told he would only receive half the fee. Scopas had taken affront to a passage in the poem in praise of Castor and Pollux. Simonides was told that he could ask the gods Castor and Pollux for the other half of the fee.

A few minutes later Simonides was called out from the banquet. He was told that two men were waiting outside for him. When he left the building he could not find anyone but, while he was outside, the roof of the banqueting hall fell in. All the guests were killed and their bodies were so badly damaged by the collapse that relatives were completely unable to identify the bodies. Simonides, however, could help the relatives because he was able to remember the places at which each of the guests has been sitting.

This is supposed to have set Simonides thinking about how the memory works, and led him to establish the first principles of the art of memory. From his experience, he reasoned that people could train their memories. He established that they would need to think of images that would represent the information they needed to remember. Then, in their minds, they would place those images in a room or building that was familiar to them. Just as he had managed to remember the positions of all the guests at the banquet, people would notice the images they had put in the room and be reminded of whatever they represented.

least bit interested that it is your house. In the bathroom a large pair of GLASSES (strange blue glasses with windscreen wipers wiping over the lenses) are sitting on the shelf with the toothbrushes. Finally you come to the bedroom, and there is a large lump underneath the bedclothes. You pull them back, and there is the biggest PUMPKIN you have ever seen.

The theory is that you can make information memorable if you put striking, unusual images in locations that you know very well. It does not have to be your house. You could place different images in different positions in your bedroom. You may want to use your body for this. One image goes on top of your head, the next dangles from your ears, the next sticks on to your nose, and so on. Use whatever location you find most suitable.

The main advantage of this system:

★ You have rather more choice about where to put your images than you do in the Peg system.

The main disadvantages of this system:

★ You would need to develop a very systematic way of walking through your house. Were you to peer into the sitting room before going into the kitchen, you might start to get all your information in the wrong order.

★ It is not as good as the Peg system if you think you might need to go straight to the fifth or eighth point on your list.

★ As with the Peg system, there is a danger of confusion if you are trying to remember too many different sets of information. While you are walking through your house looking for your images, it would be easy to run across images left in connection with a previous memory task.

Now try to remember the following keywords using the Loci system and placing these images in different places in your own home.

1. PIPE

2. DUSTBIN

3. LEATHER

4. PARSNIP

5. RAKE

6. PORCUPINE

7. MILK

8. DUSTPAN

9. PIMPLE

10. PAPER

□ **THE STORY METHOD** □

The Story method works on the basis that you create a story which links together all the keywords. It works best if the story is bizarre, surreal, impossible. It needs to be unforgettable.

You build up the images in a chain in your head, and – through the story – one image will cue the next image, which will cue the next image. As soon as you recall the first image all the others should fall into place before your mind's eye.

Now you need to make up a story that will connect all the items together in this order. Do not be inhibited. It is not going to be submitted for a short-story competition. If it sounds absolutely absurd, it is probably working particularly well as a memory device. Here is an example of the kind of story that might help you remember the information. Read it through, and you should remember all the objects in the right order.

You are in a huge BALLOON flying over the countryside. Suddenly it starts to lose height. You notice that what you had taken for a helium canister was just a HAIRDRIER. You are just being kept up by a hairdrier. The balloon starts to fall more rapidly until – plonk! splash! You have landed in the DOL-PHIN pond at a zoo. The dolphins find this hugely amusing, and together they push and toss you to the edge of the pool where there happens to be a TOWEL and some dry clothes. But you are still feeling cold and wet and badly want a shower. The only person you can ask for help is the woman in the FLOWER shop. She tells you that there are shower facilities at a GYMNASIUM just outside the zoo. So you hurry off there. You enjoy the shower, but when you start to get dressed, you just cannot face the prospect of getting into your old wet SHOES. You see a nice pair of Doc Marten's in the changing room - just the right size. They don't seem to belong to anyone and there is no one about, so you slip them on and walk out. Within minutes you are surrounded by screaming sirens. 'You're surrounded!' a voice shouts. It's the POLICE. They are on the lookout for a man who has been stealing shoes in the zoo area for several months, and they think you are their man. The chief police officer comes up to you very close, so close in fact that you can only see his GLASSES and his eyes. He pulls away from you suddenly. 'You could end up behind bars, having to eat this every day for the rest of your life,' he says, and then pulls out a large PUMPKIN from behind his back.

The main advantages of this system:

SPEECH EXERCISE

Three days after being elected President of Czechoslovakia, on New Year's Day 1990, Václav Havel made a moving address to the people of his country. Printed below is the first section of his speech. Try using the techniques described in this and the previous chapter to memorize the speech.

In the first instance it will almost certainly be helpful to break the speech down into a chain of key ideas and images. This will give you much more manageable chunks of information to commit to memory. You then need to use techniques that will relate these chunks of information to each other, which will keep the chain of ideas intact and make sure you remember them in the right order.

You may want to try using different techniques at different points in the speech. You may decide that the keywords of the first paragraph are 'flourished', 'steel', 'happy', 'trusted' and 'bright'. You may choose to create a chain of images out of these words. You may want to use the letters f, s, h, t and b to create a catch-phrase that will remind you of the words you need to remember. All the appropriate techniques described in Chapters 3 and 4 are at your disposal. Choose the most effective way for you.

My dear fellow citizens, for forty years you heard from my prede-

★ If the story is strong enough, it is very memorable.

★ You can be holding several stories in your head at the same time. It is extremely unlikely that you will start confusing one story with another.

★ You don't have to remember particular rhymes, or particular places with which to associate your keywords.

cessors on this day different variations of the same theme: how our country flourished, how many million tons of steel we produced, how happy we all were, how we trusted our government, and what bright perspectives were unfolding in front of us.

I assume you did not propose me for this office so that I, too, would lie to you.

'Our country is not flourishing. The enormous creative and spiritual potential of our nation is not being used sensibly. Entire branches of industry are producing goods which are of no interest to anyone, while we are lacking the things we need. A state which calls itself a workers' state humiliates and exploits workers. Our obsolete economy is wasting the little energy we have available. A country that once could be proud of the education level of its citizens spends so little on education that it ranks today as seventy-second in the world. We have polluted our soil, our rivers and forests, bequeathed to us by our ancestors, and we have today the most contaminated environment in Europe. Adult people in our country die earlier than in most other European countries . . .

But all this is still not the main problem. The worst thing is that we live in a contaminated moral environment. We fell morally ill because we became used to saying something different from what we thought. We learned not to believe in anything, to ignore each other, to care only about ourselves . . .'

(Taken from *The Penguin Book of Twentieth Century Speeches*, ed. Brian Macarthur.)

The main disadvantages of this system:

★ It can take some time preparing your story.

★ It is possible to remember the story, but to miss out one or two items. You should try to work out stories which make this as unlikely as possible, but there is a risk of you remembering the story in a way which loses a particular item.

Try it out for yourself with these words:

1. TOENAIL

2. FERRET

3. LASER PRINTER

4. ARMBAND

5. CURTAIN

6. LION

7. SYNAGOGUE

8. LIPS

9. SOUP

10. SHOEHORN

■ 5 ■

On the Face of It

You're standing at a party, and a woman comes up to you and starts talking to you. She is quite ordinary looking, almost nondescript. She does not work in the same profession as you. You establish that you have no friends in common, and it is entirely by accident that you are both at the same party. You are unlikely ever to meet her again. Her name – Ellen Walmsley – is a common enough name, although not one with which you have ever had any dealings before.

You speak to her for two or three minutes. She seems exactly the sort of person whose name you are likely to forget. Then just as you are about to part, she reminds you of her name and offers you £10,000 if you can remember it in six months' time. All you have to do is remember that name and you are in the money. You can bet that you won't be forgetting the name Ellen Walmsley now.

Remembering people's names is about motivation. You don't forget people's names because you have got a bad memory for names. You forget names because you are not sufficiently interested in the people. If, in the course of conversation, something happens that suddenly produces a surge of interest in you (like you are are offered a £10,000 cheque), that person becomes much more memorable.

When you struggle with someone's name, you may claim, 'Oh, I'm terribly sorry. I can't remember your name. I have a terrible memory for names.' If it is someone you meet quite often or do business with, it can be embarrassing. That's because there is a subtext. You're kidding yourself if you really believe the problem is your memory for names. You and the other person know that the truth of the matter is this: in the time that has passed since your last meeting with this person, you have not thought about him often enough to keep him in your mind. You just weren't interested in him.

It is inevitable that you forget some people. You meet thousands of people in your lifetime. In some jobs you may even meet thousands of people in a year. You cannot be equally interested in all of them, and you are bound to forget some names. You can, however, make sure that you remember the ones you need to know – even if they don't offer you £10,000. And, just by putting in a bit more effort, you can remember far more people than you would ever imagine.

For those of you who are already wondering what the upper limit is, it is very high. One president of Harvard University was able to remember the name of every student in the university. It has also been claimed that one mill manager knew every one of his eight thousand employees by name. You don't have to aim that high, but don't think you've reached perfection if you remember a couple of hundred names. You are only just beginning.

Just as it can seem rude to forget the name of someone you might be expected to remember, to remember the name of someone you would not be expected to remember is extremely impressive and very useful. The manager of that mill was not wasting his time learning eight thousand names. It is certain to have improved the feelings of the staff towards the management. The manager who knows everyone's name immediately seems more in touch with the workforce than the boss who can only name a handful of his or her senior staff. This is now taken so seriously by some major multinational companies that staff are sent on courses specifically to help them remember names.

A lot of people feel more concerned about their failure to remember names than about any other memory lapses. That is partly because of the fact that it can be socially embarrassing. It is usually easier to admit that you have to go and check up one of your facts than it is to tell someone that you can't for the life of you remember who on earth they are. It is also true, however, that remembering people's names is actually more demanding on your memory than other memory tasks. When it comes to remembering someone's name, your memory has

NAPOLEON

Napoleon's powers of memory are legendary. As a student, he applied himself to mathematics and classical literature with as much energy as to military history, and retained in his mind prodigious quantities of information. In this vast storehouse of a memory, however, he made sure he remembered the names of thousands of soldiers in his army. At the end of his life, exiled in St Helena, he is reported to have boasted to Baron Gourgaud, 'My memory is singular . . . In France I knew not only the names of the officers of all the regiments, but the places where they were recruited; I even knew the spirit that animated them.' He knew that it was important to remember the names of his officers, because a leader who knows the names of his troops commands their loyalty and respect. It was simply good generalship or, as we might call it today, good management.

PARTY TEST

Read the passage below to yourself slowly. As you read, you should try to apply some of the techniques you have learned in this chapter. You need to try to remember as much as you can about the people being described. Don't be disheartened if you find it difficult. This is one of the hardest memory tasks, but the more you practise the better you become. If need be, try reading the passage through to yourself two or three times.

You are arriving at the party. As you come in through the door, a woman in a red floral dress introduces herself as Kate Lymington. It is dark in the hallway, but she seems to have dark brown hair. She is wearing blue-rimmed glasses. You had not met her before, but she is the hostess and she takes your coat. You see your friend Alan Jacobs, over the other side of the room. He is wearing a black woollen jumper and it looks like he has lost quite a lot of weight since you last saw him about three months ago, but he needed to. He really needed to. You are just trying to catch his eye across the room, thinking of how you can comment on his weight loss in a tactful way, when a woman grabs your arm. 'I didn't know you were going to be here,' she screams. She seems a little bit drunk. You fear the worst. Yes, the shock of peroxide blonde, the Australian accent. It's Dawn.

'Come and meet the gang.' You don't have time to answer before you are being tugged into the kitchen. Dawn is shouting, 'This is him. This is the man I was telling you about.' Before you can think up any excuse at all the introductions are flying. She tells everyone your name, but it doesn't seem to make much of an impression. Their faces all look unfamiliar.

'This is Derek Kingsley.' Derek looks nervous, shy. His eyebrows join over his nose. He is smoking. He nods at you, and tells you that he works for the local authority environmental health department. 'This is Gerry Marlow.' Gerry is an older woman, short hair, crow's feet in the corners of her eyes, in trousers and a T-shirt with something written on it in Russian letters. She looks severe, but

104

seems quite friendly. She shakes your hand. She is a printer. 'Bill Diamond.' Bill has a long face, very short hair (a number two they would call it at the barber's), and an earring. He plays in a band, and he looks as if he would like making a lot of noise. His shirt is bright yellow and blue. 'Katy Bernstein': intellectual-looking, horn-rimmed spectacles, deep-set eyes, short but curly black hair, and a teacher. She seems very serious. She has a high-pitched voice. 'And Daphne Longman.' Daphne is not really paying attention. She is looking the other way, trying to get someone to pass her a can of beer. She is in jeans and a T-shirt. When she turns back you see that she has a kind of Outward Bound look to her. She's also a teacher.

At different points in the evening all these people come up to you. They expect you to remember them.

1. Who has the very short hair and earring, and is wearing the yellow and blue shirt? What is his job?

2. You need to find the hostess of the party. What is she wearing and what is her name?

3. What is the name of your old Australian friend with the peroxide blonde hair?

4. Who is the intellectual-looking girl with horn-rimmed glasses and a high-pitched voice? What does she do?

5. Who makes you think she ought to be doing Outward Bound exercises? What does she really do?

6. What is the name of your friend who has lost a lot of weight?

7. If someone were to ask whether you could see Gerry anywhere, who would you be looking for?

8. Who is the edgy-looking person whose eyebrows join up above his nose? What is his job?

three distinct tasks to perform.

★ You have to remember the name as a word.

★ You have to remember what the face looks like.

★ You have to remember the two together.

■ REMEMBERING NAMES ■

You may not think you are good at it, but remembering the names themselves is the easiest part of this memory process. The techniques you use are very similar to the techniques outlined in previous chapters. You need to look for ways of making a particular name distinctive and memorable in your mind. You need to make that name as interesting as you possibly can. That may mean making associations between the name and other words that sound the same, or it may mean looking for images that you might associate with a particular name.

□ GETTING IT STRAIGHT □

It may seem obvious but, if you want to learn someone's name, you need to make sure that you have got it straight in the first place. You have no chance of remembering the name correctly if you don't hear or register it properly. All the effort you may be making to store the name of Ms Sleeman is actually wasted if her real name is Ms Lieberman.

Listen carefully when someone is telling you their name. If you don't hear it properly, don't hesitate to ask the person to repeat it, or to check the pronunciation. However embarrassing it is to ask the person to repeat it, you are only storing up trouble for the future if you don't.

Just to make sure you've got the name, use it in the conversation. 'Well, it is interesting you should say that, Ms Lieberman, because . . .' If a sentence like that does not cause raised eyebrows, you take it as a confirmation that you are on the right name. The act of repeating it is also, in itself, likely to help you remember the name. In fact, if you don't think it sounds too odd, use the name more than once in your conversation. 'Good point, Ms Lieberman . . . I can't agree with you there, Ms Lieberman . . . Goodbye, Ms Lieberman.'

Being serious about getting your names straight also means giving yourself a little time to recite and rehearse those names once you have learned them. If you can spare a few seconds to think about the name Lieberman in the course of the evening, it could pay dividends. Of course it is not always possible, but getting one name well remembered before you move on to the next is always a good idea.

□ ORIGINS □

All names have a history, and all names have specific cultural origins. The origin of the name could well be the first thing you start thinking about as you try to reinforce the name in your head. If it is an unusual name, you might even start talking about the name. 'Ah, Oblonksy, is that a Polish name . . .?' Someone's name can be the start of a conversation about their roots. If you know why someone has a particular name, the name itself starts to become much more interesting and more memorable. His grandfather was a refugee from

STRESS

The times when you forget a business colleague's name always seem to be the times you can least well afford to forget it. Mr What'shisname may not have been very interesting and he may not have made a very big impression on you personally, but he was a terribly important business contact. You were certainly motivated enough to remember his name. You were hypermotivated, but it seems to have gone clean out of your head.

It is all a question of balance. While motivation is important, if you crank up your motivation too much you are under stress. And stress is bad for your memory, really bad. Under stress, the blood starts racing round your brain, your fingers start to fidget, and your concentration falters. One research project showed that nurses working in intensive care have more memory lapses than their colleagues in other hospital departments. Eyewitnesses to crimes are notoriously fallible witnesses, and even experienced actors can suffer stage fright. In the same way if you're inside that important business meeting and you start to feel the palms of your hands getting sweaty, you know there is a risk that your memory is not working as well as it could be.

It's time for a three-point plan:

● Make sure you are breathing regularly and deeply.

● Relax your body and your shoulders so that you don't feel so tensed up.

● Believe in yourself. You're doing fine, and worrying about it won't help you at all.

Warsaw. Her name is actually quite common in Nigeria. His name is a traditional Shropshire name that you don't often find in any other part of the country.

It is not only the obscure name that may have interesting or memorable origins, however. 'Fitz' only means 'son of', but there is a fair chance that anyone with a name that starts Fitz- (e.g. Fitzroy, Fitzclarence) is descended from an illegitimate branch of the royal family. These families very often attached the prefix 'Fitz' to their surnames. Many people's names indicate a profession or trade that was presumably how their ancestors earned a living. Baker, Taylor, Farmer and Merchant are all common enough surnames that almost certainly indicate the origins of the person concerned. Her father may have been a grocer, but Margaret Thatcher's ancestors were almost certainly climbing up medieval scaffolding to thatch roofs.

☐ COMPARE ☐

To know thirty-five people with the surname Burton may start to get confusing, but to know more than one will actually be helpful. It will help you build up associations. When you meet someone called Burton, you can compare that person with your other Burton friends.

The associations you make do not have to be associations with your own friends. This new person that you are meeting could remind you of the actor Richard Burton. Alternatively he could be so unlike Richard Burton that the very fact of them having the same name strikes you as absurd. Absurdities are easily remembered.

It is always worth while scanning your brain for any other people of the same name of whom you have heard or who you know. It is possible that someone with a surname Fowler might make you think of a former politician or the leading family of a soap opera. Someone you meet called Morrison might bring to mind a supermarket chain in the North of

England or a famous rock star. Make the most of how this new information is going to fit in with the material that is already stored in your brain.

□   **WORD PLAY**   □

It is an act of politeness to get a name right when you are speaking to someone, but no one knows what you do with the name when it is in your head. You can take it apart, make jokes out of it, find an odd rhyme for it, and no one will be offended. People called Bottomley, Darling and Pratt may suspect that their names are not always taken terribly seriously, but they will have learned to live with it. Other people will suspect nothing.

It is easiest to find associations for people whose names have a particular meaning. Peacock, Fox, Green, Waters and Castle all immediately suggest associations. There are also names like Bromley, London, Bradford, Carlisle and Bristol which don't make huge demands on your imagination. You must not, however, feel defeated if nothing springs to mind immediately. Start thinking laterally.

It may help you remember the name of Kevin Gatt, if you are consciously aware of the fact that his name rhymes with 'rat' or 'brat'. You might remember Mr Cotton better if you rhyme him with the word 'rotten'. Alternatively Pakenham becomes Pack-'em-in (particularly appropriate if the person concerned has a large appetite), Gopal becomes Go-Pal (especially good for a fast runner), or Lazenby becomes Laze-on-beach.

PHOTOFIT

No one needs us to improve our memory for faces more than the police. For centuries they have been chasing suspects with only the vaguest and most general descriptions on which to work. For the last thirty years they have been using systems like Identikit and Photofit in an effort to get more specific evidence from witnesses; but these identification systems have not lived up to expectations.

Photofit was invented in the early 1970s, and within a few years it had crept into everyone's vocabulary. It was based on sets of photographs of different features. Witnesses had to build up a picture of the suspect by picking and combining the appropriate features. The idea seemed promising enough, but most research tests have given it the thumbs down. Although it was quite good at recreating the general type of face, it very rarely gave anything approaching a close likeness. The more skilled and sensitive the Photofit operator, the closer the likeness achieved, but very often witnesses' verbal accounts provided a more accurate description.

Part of the problem seems to be that systems like Photofit require witnesses to examine individual features in isolation; but, even when you know someone very well it is not easy to create an image of the mouth separated from the rest of the face. When you have only ever caught a fleeting glimpse of the person, it is almost impossible.

An electronic version of Photofit called E-Fit (or Electronic Facial Identification Technique) is now available and should address the most serious problems. In the first instance witnesses can change the shapes and sizes of the features themselves. Secondly they can see a picture build up in front of them, and are able to keep changing and reshaping features until they are satisfied. All the features are seen as part of a composite face.

■ REMEMBERING FACES ■

Remembering faces is considerably more complex than merely remembering the names. Occasionally one person may look a bit like someone else you know; but, as a rule, you can't rhyme one pair of eyes with another, and you can't say an awful lot about a person's genealogy by looking at their ears. When you try to store a face in your brain, it is not like memorizing a name, speech or a shopping list.

Some psychologists even believe that we remember faces in a completely different way from anything else. There is a rare brain condition called prosopagnosia. Sufferers have no sight problems and no difficulty in recognizing objects, but they are completely unable to recognize people whom they may have known for years.

The rest of us manage passably well when it comes to recognizing people we know well, but we are not all that good at recalling vivid pictures of them in our minds and are very poor at describing them. Could you describe even your own face in such a way that would enable a stranger to come and pick you out from a crowd of a hundred? It would not be easy.

□ SPECIAL FEATURES □

Two rings through the nose, a pink spiky haircut, and a birthmark on the forehead, and you are probably home and dry. Provided she does not remove the nose rings and dye her hair again, this is someone you are likely to remember.

Of course not everyone has got features quite as distinctive as these, but most people have something slightly idiosyncratic about their face. Caricaturists can find that kind of feature in every face. Even hidden behind the most nondescript of people there may lurk a protruding jaw, buck teeth, or a nose that is slightly askew.

There is a skill to finding that giveaway feature in every face; but the harder you look the more you will find, and these kinds of features will pay dividends when it comes to remembering faces. Look hard for them. If you can spot them, they are the quickest short cut available.

☐   **A FACIAL GRAMMAR**   ☐

You know there are differences between the mouth of Mr Capstick and the mouth of Mr Smith, but you cannot find a way of putting those differences into words. Perhaps it is that Mr Capstick's mouth seems to turn up a bit at the corners, but there again Mr Smith's mouth can do just that as well. Perhaps it is that Mr Capstick's upper lip is a bit tighter and thinner, but when you look again, you are not quite sure.

The oldest system of improving memory for faces is based on the idea that we really need to develop a grammar for faces. We need to be able to break down and build up faces in the same way as we break down and build up sentences. This is the basic principle behind Leonardo da Vinci's system (see page 124), Photofit pictures (see page 111) and countless other systems. Some theorists encourage you to break up the face into different visual units. Others think it is a question of becoming more confident in the way you use words to describe a face.

Essentially you have to start to classify all the features of someone as soon as you meet that person. While you are talking to Mr Capstick, you are busy running through a

Can you work out to whom these six pairs of famous eyes belong? Turn over the page to see how many you got right.

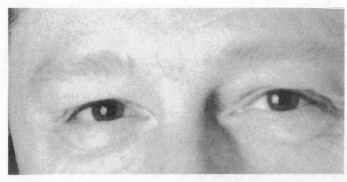

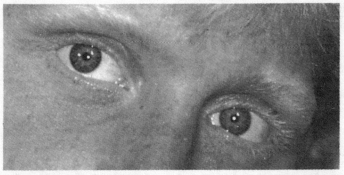

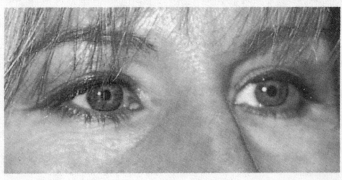

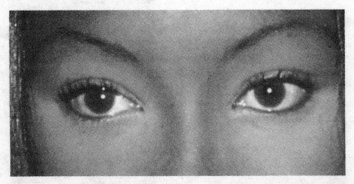

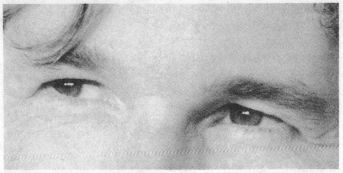

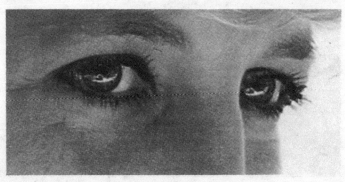

It's not always as easy as you think. Did you manage to guess these six stars?

Bill Clinton

Boris Becker

Barbara Streisand

Naomi Campbell

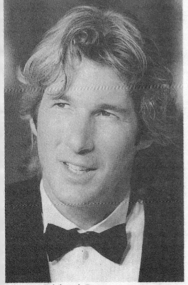

Richard Gere

Princess Diana

checklist of characteristics for each of his features. Is his hair spiky, wavy, crewcut, straight, thinning, parted, curly, medium, long? Are his eyelashes thick or thin, long or short? And so on.

There may have been some virtues in this system for Renaissance artists wanting to create a model of their subject's face or for police trying to trace suspects. It may even help some people remember faces. Most recent evidence, however, suggests that this is of limited value.

In the first instance you have to make an extremely complex list of judgements in what might seem to be a very short time. It might start to get difficult to concentrate on what Mr Capstick was saying if you were trying to check out the thickness of his eyebrows at the same time.

Secondly, we don't actually look at people as a compilation of different features. In fact if you break someone's face down into a set of separate features, they may no longer be recognizable at all. What makes a face distinctive is not so much the individual isolated features, but the way those features all work together to form particular expressions. This, of course, also begins to tell you more about their personality. Is it a face that tends to frown, or twitch, or laugh, or look vague and absent-minded? At the end of the day these are questions that you will only be able to answer by looking at the whole face, and these are also the kinds of issue that are likely to make a face more memorable for you. By asking these sorts of questions you are starting to get more interested in the person, and that is the most important thing of all.

☐ **FIND OUT ABOUT THE PERSON** ☐

All recent psychological research suggests that you are much better off getting to know a person than you are ticking boxes on your mental checklist of physical attributes. The more interested you become in someone's personality, history, likes and dislikes, the better you will remember his name and his face.

Your first job, then, is to find out more about the person you want to remember. You don't need to cross-examine him, but take an interest in what he does, what he likes and how he reacts to things. The kind of information that helps you distinguish him from other people as a person is also going to help you distinguish his face.

Then, as soon as you can, start to make some preliminary value judgements. They can be temporary judgements and you can change them as you get to know him better, but they should be strong judgements. The quicker you can sort out in your own head what you think of a person, the quicker you will begin to remember him or her. Sometimes you immediately find someone arrogant, charming, pompous or hilarious. Take advantage of your own immediate feelings about him. If you don't pass judgements quite so quickly, ask yourself a few questions about this person. Would you like to go on holiday with him? Would you feel safe if he offered you a lift in his car? Would you like to work with him, or for him, or have him work for you? Ask any questions which are going to reveal to yourself more of your own instinctive feelings about this person. These feelings are going to help you remember him.

Then make a conscious effort to relate your feelings about this person to his physical attributes (you have almost certainly already done this subconsciously). Of course not everyone looks like their character. Someone who is mean and stingy is not necessarily thin, tightlipped and tense. Someone who is gentle and caring does not necessarily have soft and rounded features. Nonetheless, faces do carry a lot of people's personalities. You can see happiness in a face, and you can see trouble and tension. If you start to expand outwards and look not just at a face, but at someone's posture, bearing, mannerisms and expressions, you are getting very close to the character of the person. You are certainly looking at some of the features which will have influenced your character judgements in the first place.

■ PUTTING NAMES TO FACES ■

The more interested you have become in someone the less trouble you will have in fitting the name to the face. It will have become important to you to remember the two together, so you will do so. The more you can do to build up your interest in a person, the less of a problem this will be.

There is no need to pretend, however, that some people won't just slip through the net. We have all been in places when we recognize people, we know that we know their names, but just can't put the two together at the crucial moment. In an emergency, you can use the 'tip-of-the-tongue' strategies outlined in Chapter 1 of this book; but, for the time being, let's aim high. Let's try and prevent it happening in the first place.

★ Don't miss the obvious. In fiction it is a common enough occurrence for characters to have names which reflect their personality traits or looks. Dickens peoples his novels with Gradgrinds, Boffins, Pickwicks, Podsnaps and Fledgebys. In the world of entertainment people change their names to fit the kind of image they want to cut with the general public. For rock stars Bob Dylan sounds better than Robert Zimmerman, Elvis Costello better than Declan McManus and Sting better than Gordon Sumner, while John Lydon found fame as Johnny Rotten. They all took names which were supposed to make them more memorable, and to suit a particular identity. Sometimes, however, names just happen to fit neatly – or at least it is possible to make them fit neatly.

Do you know someone called Singh who has got a good singing voice, or looks as if her eyebrows have been singed? Do you know someone called Piper who has big blown-out cheeks, someone called Jemson who is in the jewellery trade, or someone called Katz who keeps mogs? The number of people who can be remembered like this may be limited, but don't miss the most obvious of memory opportunities.

★ Visualize. If you cannot find a completely transparent link between the name and the person, you are going to have to start using your imagination. This does require some effort on your part, so you should limit the use of this technique to situations where you really need to remember someone's name. There are obviously going to be occasions when it is perfectly reasonable for you not to bother remembering a name, and occasions when you can remember names without creating special pictures in your mind.

Where you do need another trick up your sleeve, however, you can use your imagination. Let's say that Piper does not have full blown-out cheeks, does not play the pipes and does not

Looking at these twelve faces and corresponding names for no more than two minutes, can you remember the right name for the right face?

Hilary Kalopsidiotis Gary Debrowski

Jennifer Fry Frank Pinart

Ken Samuel Sally Thompson

Jackie Henderson
Lee Conyers
Maureen Sturgeon

John Allgrove
Sanchia Cecconi
David Leovold

smoke a pipe. On the face of it you might think you are in trouble, but far from it. Now you start to imagine a pipe sticking out of his mouth and billowing clouds of blue smoke, or you imagine his nose in the shape of a pipe, or a piece of pipe tubing sticking out of his ear.

Think what you might do to conjure up images for a Jemson who did not work as a jeweller or a Katz who hated cats. Even less immediately promising names can be broken up or altered in ways that will help you find visual images. Radford could

DA VINCI SYSTEM

In his *Treatise on Painting*, the Renaissance artist Leonardo da Vinci addressed the problem of having to reproduce likenesses of people who were not prepared to be artists' models. He developed a sixteenth-century version of the Photofit picture.

He advised artists to make up a set of drawings of different features in a notebook. Under da Vinci's system the face was divided into four main features – the nose, the mouth, the chin, and the forehead. For each of these features there was a large, but finite, number of possible variations. The nose, for example, had to be examined both in profile and head-on. Viewed in profile

there were several different possible noses: straight, bunched, concave, raised in a hump above the mid point of the nose, raised up below the mid point of the nose, aquiline, flat, round, and sharp. A further eleven categories of nose differentiate the head-on perspectives. Beyond this there were more categories for all the other features.

Once the artist had built up this huge library of features, the notebook could be used as a reference book. When you caught sight of your subject you could mark up which of these features were appropriate, and then return to the drawing in your studio.

become associated with Radio 4, or with Bradford, or with a red Ford motor car. Billingham could be associated with an invoice sandwiched between two large pieces of ham. The next stage is to link those images in memorable ways to the faces you need to remember. All you need to do is imagine Radford hurtling towards you in his red Ford, and Billingham sinking his teeth into this unusual sandwich. If you can start to do this memorably and confidently, the battle is won. The names that you need to be remembered are going to be lodged in your mind in a distinctive way.

■ 6 ■

Making it Memorable

You may have worked hard at all the techniques described in the previous chapters. You may now be able to remember the names of people you meet at parties. You may be better at remembering the key points of books that you read. And you may be able to sit through an extremely dull lecture and still be able to remember the contents of it three months later. But, just because you can do it, don't assume that everyone else can.

Your memory may now be quite skilful at turning phrases into images, restructuring arguments, and reorganizing all the new information it receives. If you are talking to someone, it is possible that she will be applying some of these techniques herself; but the chances are that she is not. Seconds after you begin to get boring you will see a glazed look coming across her face, and her attention drifting away from you. If you want her to remember what you are saying, you cannot afford to leave it totally up to her. You have to make your points as memorable as possible.

There are going to be any number of occasions when it will be useful to you to use your understanding of memory to make an impact on other people's memories. We live in an age which is teeming with information. It is a world of memos, and papers, and talks, and meetings. We are all so used to being bombarded with information that we often allow information to come in one ear and go straight out of the other. If you don't want this to happen to your information, you need to think about what will make it most memorable. You might be in a meeting, and need to make sure the points you are making are remembered by everyone sitting round the table. You might even be in a job interview, for which you know there are fifteen other applicants being interviewed the same day. You have to make yourself and your ideas stand out. You might be writing a report and need to make sure that your readers really take the key points on board.

Understanding memory is not, in itself, a guaranteed passport to success in all these situations. It is also important that you develop the confidence to speak in public, that you get your breathing right and that you don't stand rigidly on a stage hiding behind your notes. Nonetheless, what you have learned about the workings of your own memory is enormously helpful in giving you clues to what will make an impression on other people's.

The techniques described in Chapters 3 and 4 involved organizing information in a lateral and seemingly bizarre manner. You were encouraged to use Number–Letter codes and to create the strangest of visual images in your own mind. You may not want to go as far as this when you are giving other people information. It might seem odd to publicize an embarrassing rhyme, to give your audience details of how you associate inflation with a Chelsea bun, or to dye your hair pink for an interview for an office job. Even if you don't take them to the same extremes, however, the general principles remain the same. The key ways of making sure you are remembered are:

HOW TO BE BORING

Imagine you were giving a speech and you wanted to bore your audience into a stupor. You wanted to write and deliver your speech in a way which would be so dull that no one would remember a word of it the moment your speech was over. You wanted to see eyelids drooping as soon as you started to speak. You wanted to hear snoring coming from the back row, and see people across the hall talking to each other about completely different subjects in groups of two or three. You wanted this to be the most boring speech ever.

Now think about what you would need to do to have that effect on people.

● You want the subject to be one in which the audience has no prior interest at all. Talk to an audience of Jason Donovan fans about astro-physics, or a group of university lecturers about soap operas.

● Just in case one or two of them start to get interested in the subject, make sure they cannot understand what you are saying properly anyway. You can do this by using jargon. If you go on long enough about Michelle Fowler or Emily Bishop without explaining who they are, even the best intentioned of the university lecturers will start to lose concentration. They won't know what you are going on

★ Make sure the information is not boring for the audience. That really means making sure the information relates to your audience. We are all most likely to forget information that we find boring and that does not seem to relate to us very well.

★ Organize information well. The more tidily you can present your information, the easier it will be to file away in your mind. Think of everybody – like yourself – having memories that are like overworked libraries. If you want to give people a better chance of putting your information away in its proper place, about, and, however hard they listen, they will never really be able to find out. You will never explain the basics.

● Talk in a monotone. If you can keep your voice so quite that it is barely audible, so much the better. If not, make sure you never alter the pitch or speed of you voice. Read from sheets of paper. Don't look up at the audience at all. Keep your eyes firmly fixed on your script.

● Ramble. However dull it is, a logical, orderly presentation of facts can become interesting to some people. If you digress wildly and keeping going off at tangents, you should manage to throw people off. The best way to do this is to make sure you don't over-prepare your thoughts. If you just wander into the hall and start talking without planning your speech, you should be OK.

● Go on for a long time. Some people have extraordinarily good powers of concentration. However hard you try, these people may be able to hold out for quite some time. But rest assured, if you go on and on and on for long enough, even those with high levels of concentration will eventually start to drift off.

Of course if you wanted to give a speech in which you wanted your audience to be sitting on the edges of their seats and taking in everything you said, you would avoid . . . no, I don't think I need to say it. The point's been made.

you need to present it to them in a well-organized and well-labelled form. It has got to be clear from the outset where your information should be filed in their brains.

★ Present the information in a way that will make it stand out in people's minds. The kind of images you created in Chapter 4 of this book may be a bit too extreme and obscure when you are trying to get information across to other people; but you should still be looking for ways that will make your information as striking as possible.

■ KEEPING IT RELEVANT ■

Think about your audience. Don't ever stop thinking about your audience. Whether your audience is sitting in an armchair reading your letter, sitting opposite you in a meeting, or massed in an auditorium as you hold forth to hundreds of people, your audience is always human. It is not a tape recorder that will go on recording your information whatever happens. It may have some interest in the subject, but it will also have a lot of other things on its mind. One slip and it will be thinking about the film on television last night, the possible outcome of the FA Cup final, or shopping that has to be bought on the way home from work.

You need to make a pitch for your audience. It is a good sign that they have actually turned up in the first place, or that they are bothering to read your report. Nonetheless, you are in competition for that audience. You're in competition with all the other unconnected thoughts that could enter their heads. On the face of it a lot of those thoughts may seem more interesting than your subject. So you've got a battle on.

If you are to have any chance at all, you must make sure you are pitching your information at the right level. You need to make sure you are answering or at least addressing the kind of questions that will interest your audience. If you think you've got a catch-all lecture that will work for everyone, take a very close look at it. You could end up losing everyone. A talk about the history of Skipton Castle will depend on whether you are talking to a group of eight-year-old children, a party of American tourists, or a local history association. If your talk keeps one of those groups absolutely spellbound, the chances are that it will bore the other two groups rigid.

Of course the interest of your audience does relate to the

subject to a certain extent. You can bet that ears will prick up if you are telling office staff about a new way to claim more money in overtime payments or about a plan to offer longer holidays. Nonetheless, no subject is a write-off. However dull it may seem, there is sure to be a way of getting people to keep reading or to keep listening.

Always ask yourself whether your information is presented in a way that makes it relate as closely as possible to your audience's concerns. You may know it is relevant and important information, but they may need convincing (or at least reminding) that this information really matters to them.

SPEECH TEST

Based on what you have learned from this book, prepare three five-minute speeches about memory improvement. It's a good way for you to revise the information, but it is also a chance to think about ways in which you can make your speech memorable.

Each of the speeches should be for a different audience. One might be a speech to a group of students wanting advice on how to prepare for examinations. One speech might be for a bridge club whose members want to improve their memories for cards. One speech might be for a group of elderly people who wanted to be reassured that old age does not mean they have to worry about memory failures.

Write speeches which will encourage each of your audiences to try out new memory techniques. Think in particular about the key points you want to cover and how those points are specifically relevant to your audience. Also make sure you work hard at the opening to your speech. You establish your relationship with your audience in the first minute or two. If you get things wrong at the beginning, it is very hard to make up the ground.

Address your audience very directly. You could start a health and safety speech by pitching straight into a description of a potential emergency. You could start like this:

'You are at your desk finishing a report for a 5 p.m. deadline. There is a smell of burning coming from the other side of the room. It's an acrid smell, but it is fairly faint and no one else in the room seems too troubled by it . . .'

By creating the kind of situation in which your audience could actually find themselves you are beginning to engage them. At the same time you are making them use their visual imaginations. They are being asked to form pictures in their minds, and those pictures are much more likely to be remembered than your words. This kind of opening is much more likely to win their attention than if you were to start:

'As a result of the incident on the fourth floor of the head office building, Regulation 631B has now been changed. From now on it will be incumbent on the safety officer of each building to note all obstructions that are reported . . .'

Think of ways in which you can build up the interest level of your audience. It may be that the information you have to reveal is not all that interesting in its own right. You know that, but your audience does not. It's worth trying to build up an element of mystery and intrigue. Try to get them fired up and motivated to find out that information. Then, when it comes – even if it is not exactly earth-shattering information – they will be so eager to find out that they will be all ears. An opening like this can get you off to a good start.

'This information is something that has been kept secret from us for over eighteen months. Quite a lot of people on high would still prefer us to be kept in the dark about it. But it is something that affects every single person in this room and it could mean the difference between life and death . . .'

MARK TWAIN'S LECTURE TIPS

Mark Twain was a prolific lecturer. He toured all over Europe and the United States giving lectures on all manner of subjects, but he never got lazy about those lectures. They were always well planned and entertaining. And they were geared not only to the background but even to the mood of his audience.

This is how he described his system:

Any lecture of mine ought to be a running narrative plank, with square holes in it, six inches apart, all the length of it, and then in my mental shop I ought to have plugs (half marked 'serious' and the others marked 'humorous') to select from and jam into these holes according to the temper of the audiences.

(from *The Love Letters of Mark Twain*, ed. Dixon Wecter.)

You do have to be careful not to let this drag on too long, not to overhype your subject to the point that it becomes untrue (or ridiculous), but it is worth pulling all the tricks out of the bag if you really want people to remember what you are saying. Your audience are most likely to remember information that they are most motivated to remember.

■ ORGANIZATION ■

Decide what you want to say, and organize your thoughts accordingly. You need to be clear and to the point, and to select the information that people really need. It's much better to make three points well and clearly than it is to make thirty points that everyone will forget. If you have to say goodbye to an interesting anecdote or a clever turn of phrase, don't worry.

VISUAL AIDS

When you are giving a talk, visual aids can be enormously useful. They are a way of highlighting information. A few words on a flip chart can be the reference point for your audience through the course of the whole speech. It can provide a permanently visible outline so that it can always be seen that every point you make fits into the overall scheme of things. A good map can save you a thousand words (and so help keep your speech short and simple). A chart can sometimes have the kind of impact that makes it the key to how people remember the whole talk you have given.

Think about the range of visual aids that you could use – overhead projector, slides, handout leaflets, photographs, blackboard, exhibits. If any of these could be useful to you, make sure you get hold of them. Be certain, however, that they are really going to help you make your points. Appropriate visual aids can be very effective, but they are not useful as props for you to hide behind nor as meaningless gimmicks. Inappropriate visual aids are confusing. However picturesque they look, no one wants to

Over and above anything else you need a clear objective. You have to be sure of your key points yourself before you can expect anyone else to get a clear message.

You know why your information is important. It may be filed away in your head under 'Good ideas to save the company from imminent collapse', or under 'Good ideas to secure a better future for everyone employed by the company'. If you want everyone else to remember it, you need to make sure your audience knows where it is supposed to keep the information as well. You need to make sure your information is structured in a sensible and memorable way, and that it is laid out clearly and well labelled. If you are writing a document this may mean be shown a set of slides that aren't really related to the speech. A chart that includes a huge amount of complex detail is more likely to be confusing than helpful. Good visual aids are simple, direct and relevant.

In exactly the same way think about the way you space out your paragraphs and how you use different typefaces and **type-sizes** when you are drawing up a report. Many computer printers will give you the facility to use a whole range of different styles. Test them out, and see if they give you the opportunity to highlight <u>crucial words</u> in the text. You will obviously be looking for a style that is appropriate to the document you are writing. You might not want to keep changing the typeface of a novel, but it could be very useful if you were drawing up a document for a union meeting or a school parent–teacher association meeting. Words that are bolder or larger or in a different typeface will leap out at the reader. They will be the words that your readers remember long after they have put the document down. Be warned again, however, not to change style simply for effect. Varying **typesize** or **typeface** is effective when used to highlight a key point, but it is just distracting when done for its own sake.

providing section headings. If you are giving a talk, it may mean that you have to recap on your key points so that your audience is clear about how your ideas fit together and why you are giving them the information in the first place.

■ MAKING IT STAND OUT ■

The whole of Chapter 4 was about how you could form effective images, visual associations and narratives which, by virtue of their strangeness, would help you remember information. When you are presenting information to other people, you cannot be quite as lateral or obscure as you are when you memorize information for yourself. Nonetheless, it is always a good idea to see if there is a striking visual image or an unlikely comparison, which might make information stand up in the minds of your audience.

It may not be all that exciting to tell your workforce that over 23 million of the company's widgets have now been sold worldwide over the last twelve months. It might be much more memorable if you were to tell them that the number of widgets sold was enough to fill every room in the Empire State Building from floor to ceiling twice over. The number of widgets sold is the equivalent of one widget for every single household in Britain. More people now own these widgets than own electric kettles. Whatever you say has to be true, but if you can find an unlikely (and, if possible, visually striking) way of presenting information, it is more likely to stay in people's minds.

Simple graphic illustrations can be an enormous help in getting people to remember what you are saying to them. They can act as mental cues which will bring back to your audience the key points that you have been trying to make. It is much easier for people to call up images from their memories, than it is for them to remember complicated arguments and detailed statistics.

There is no magic formula to making information memorable. Advertising agencies and public relations companies are always trying out new ways to be so shocking, so surprising, and so inventive that we cannot fail to remember the products they are trying to sell us. New techniques, however, become old hat very quickly. As soon as the ideas are more commonplace they stop having the same effect on audiences. In the same way you can't afford to become complacent about your style of presentation. If you really want people to remember your information, you need to keep on re-applying what you have learned about memory. The principles should stay the same, but the end result should always be changing. For each presentation you make, you need to think afresh about your audience and your subject matter. You need to be constantly on the lookout for ways of presenting it that are different, fresh and striking enough to stand out in the already overcrowded memories of your audience.

Bibliography

Baddeley, Alan
Memory: A User's Guide
(Penguin Books)
This is a classic and very well-written book on how the memory works. The first edition was written in 1982, but it was updated for a new edition in 1993.

Buzan, Tony
The Mind Map Book: Radiant Thinking
(BBC Books, 1993)
Strong on techniques that will help you use your memory more effectively. Buzan has written a large number of very accessible books on how to use your memory more effectively.

Gruneberg, Michael
Linkword series of books to help in the rapid learning of a vocabulary and basic grammar of a foreign language, using the mnemonic techniques described in Chapter 4. Available for French, Spanish, German, Italian, Greek and Portuguese, each of these books will give you a basic vocabulary of about 400 words. (Corgi Books)

Lorayne, Harry
How to Develop a Superpower Memory
(Thorsons, 1993)

Luria, A. R.
The Mind of a Mnemonist
(Harvard University Press, 1987)
This is the story of Shereshevski and his extraordinary powers of memory.

O'Brien, Dominic
How to Develop a Perfect Memory
(Pavilion Books, 1993)
An account of the techniques used by World Memory champion, Dominic O'Brien.

Rose, Steven
The Making of Modern Memory
(Bantam Press, 1992)
An extremely readable account of the cellular mechanisms of memory by neuroscientist and Professor of Biology, Steven Rose.

Index